# Wounds

## to

# Wisdom...

## The Survivor Series

## Volume 1

Compiled by Best-selling Author Tamiko Lowry-Pugh

Written by 12 Bold and Courageous Domestic Violence Survivors

Published by the Johnson Tribe Publishing House, LLC
Atlanta, GA

Johnson Tribe Publishing House
P.O. Box 1587 Powder Springs Georgia 30127
info@johnsontribepublishing.com
www. JohnsonTribePublishing.com


Manufactured in the United States of America
10 9 8 7 6 5 4 3 2 1

FIRST EDITION – February 2016
Creative Direction: Tamiko Lowry-Pugh
Book Design: Stacey Bowers, August Pride, LLC
Cover Photo Credit: Cornell McBride, McBride Photography


ISBN-13: 978-0-9896733-9-6

USA $19.95
Canada $21.50

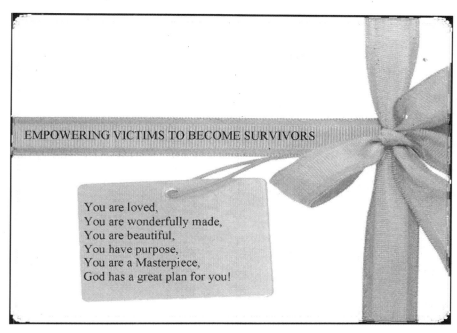

EMPOWERING VICTIMS TO BECOME SURVIVORS

You are loved,
You are wonderfully made,
You are beautiful,
You have purpose,
You are a Masterpiece,
God has a great plan for you!

# THIS BOOK HAS BEEN GIFTED TO

_____

# FROM

_____

# ON

_____

For the blessings of true survivorship in all areas of your life.

# *Dedication*

This book is dedicated to all of the survivors in the world.
There is purpose behind the pain. God will turn your wounds into
wisdom and one day you will say

"Wow; I Survived!"

No matter what it is you go through in life, remember that all things
work together for the good for those who love God and who are called
according to his purpose.

Romans 8:27-29

# Acknowledgements

My Heavenly Father: Thank you for the life lessons that gave me strength and perseverance on this journey of life. Thank you for the vision, the mission, and the calling that you have placed in my life to empower victims to become survivors. Thank you for allowing me to turn my wounds into wisdom and my pain into purpose. *Because of you,* I survived! You alone are my rock and my salvation. You are my fortress. I shall not be moved. *Psalm 62:2.*

Co-authors: Thank you for being brave, bold, and courageous enough to share your stories. Thank you for being transparent, and for trusting me with something so precious. Your stories will breathe hope into those going through what you survived. And for that, I say thank you!

Kenny Pugh: Thank you for being my 'number one fan' …as you always say. You inspire me to be greater in all areas of life.

Destiny & Michael: Thank you for being the most supporting children a mom could have. Thank you for supporting my dreams and being apart of the vision. You are truly the reason why I work so hard.

Dr. Adair White-johnson: Thank you for believing in this project from the moment I mentioned it to you. Thank you for your professionalism, expertise, and commitment to seeing this project through via Johnson Tribe Publishing House.

Knowingly, I Survived...

I survived because I was wonderfully made with a purpose.

I survived because through that purpose; I will fulfill my destiny.

I survived because I know who I am.

# Contents

Stand strong by realizing your vision, understanding your calling, overcoming your obstacles and pursuing your passions.

~Tamiko Lowry Pugh

# WOUND

. . . . .

## MERRIAM-WEBSTER DEFINES A WOUND AS

An injury in which the surface of something is torn, pierced, cut, or otherwise broken. Hurt.

He heals the brokenhearted and binds up their wounds.

Psalm 147:3

"The human race tends to remember the abuses to which it has been subjected rather than the endearments. What's left of kisses? Wounds, however, leave scars."

— Bertolt Brecht

# Preface

Though Wounded, I Was Not Destroyed...
I Survived!

Think of a young child playing on a playground. As she runs, jumps and climbs she is so filled with the joy of interacting with the other children that the excitement of the moment brings laughter to her spirit and a smile on her face. So of course, she doesn't consider that she will get hurt.

Then suddenly, another child comes over and pushes her down (mistakenly or intentional). She falls to the ground badly scraping her knee which causes her so much pain that she begins to cry. Naturally, her mother runs to her aid to console her; cleaning the wound, carefully bandaging it. Then over time, nurturing the wound until it one day heals.

However, as she grew older, the scar remained as a reminder of that day on the playground. Though she tried everything that she could to try to make it fade nothing has ever made it disappear. So, she just frustratingly conceals it.

Many of us are like the little girl in the story, throughout the course of our lives we are often faced with many situations and circumstances that may cause us to become wounded—physically, emotionally, mentally, financially and even spiritually. These bumps and bruises we tend to carry with us along our journey; which seem to never go away.

*Identify:// Generally,* when we speak of *wounds* we tend to gravitate toward thinking about only the physical wounds. However, we must consider that we are made up of more than just physical mass. Therefore, wounding may occur as matters of the heart (*emotional*), matters of the mind (*mental*), matters of the soul (*spiritual*) or matters of our livelihood (*financial*)—all of which can affect our overall wellness. By properly identifying with all areas of your life you will begin to discover the essential tools needed along your journey toward the peacefulness of true survivorship.

*Source:// It's* important that we take full responsibility for examining the anatomy of our wounds so that we will grasp ahold of and embrace the true power of our healing and wellness. Gaining an understanding of the source of our wounds also helps us to become more aware of *"clear-and-present-danger"*. In other words, by recognizing repetitive source patterns, we become more mindful of our choices in the present.

Though our wounds may derive from many sources [intentional or unintentional] and in some cases have a lingering painful effect, they serve as learning scars that teach us throughout our journey to wisdom.

I will stand strong in the midst of my challenges and struggles because I believe in my future.

I survived!

# Chapter One

## BLINDED BY LOVE
By Colvina Colvin

Love is blind, and love can be foolish – Our heart doesn't always love
the right people at the right time. Sometimes we hurt the ones that
love us the most, and sometimes we love the ones that don't deserve
our love at all. ~Uknown

I remember it like it was yesterday. It was in the early 80's, and while
walking through the Main Place Mall, a guy named "MC" approached
me. He was very charming with one of the best smiles I had ever
seen. He said all the right things and he told me that I was beautiful
and that I should be a model. As time progressed, I discovered that he
told that to all the ladies that he came in contact with.  But the
difference was that I believed him.  This was his main tactic to "get
his girls." Anyway, I gave him my number and not long after that; we
were dating. After dating for a few months, things began to get a little
more serious. I met his mom and family, and he met mine.

What I liked most about MC was his infectious smile because
it seemed to make everything "okay." He also knew how to say the
right things to stroke my ego and make me feel safe and secure.

Despite all of this, it did not take long before MC started to
show his jealous ways. Of course, when a man is jealous we

sometimes think that means that he really cares about us. And that's what I initially thought. He was so jealous that he did not want me out of his sight. I remember being out with him and I ran into an old male friend who gave me a hug. MC did not like that, and it made him furious. It got to the point where if he saw me talking to someone of the opposite sex, he would get angry and accuse me of wanting to be with that person.

I also remember him asking me to stop taking my birth control pills so that I could have his baby. But there was no way that I was going to allow that to happen. I pretended to stop taking the pills but was still taking them all along. When he found out that I was still taking the pills, he cursed me out and began to brutally attack me.

The arguments and fights continued for months. After he would attack me each time, he would say how sorry he was and that it would never happen again. And then he would want to have sex with me. This made me feel disgusting, but I felt as though I had to do it in order to make him happy.

There were so many times when I ran out of the house with my toddler daughter, running down the street with nothing but my night clothes on. Many asked why I didn't leave him and all that I could say was that it was because I "loved him." Well, when you think you love someone, or you think they love you, you believe that things will eventually get better. Or you become so accustomed to it that you accept it as part of the relationship.

His mom was a very loving woman. At one point she allowed me and my daughter to move in with her because I had nowhere else to go. I really loved his mom as though she were my own mom. We still keep in touch almost 40 years later. Although his mom was a sweetheart, and she really loved my daughter and me, she could not control her son's outbursts. There were times when he would attack me in front of her, and she could not stop him.

As always, MC would "sweet talk" me into returning home to stay with him. He did not work, and I was receiving public assistance at the time. Whenever my monthly check would arrive, we would always have another fight because e said that I would "act funny" when I had a little money in my pocket.

There were also times when he would get so angry that he would just kick me without provocation, and there were times when he would throw me out of the house without shoes on during the cold winter months.

One day MC decided to leave and moved to Washington, DC without much notice. That should have been my opportunity to get my life together without him. But I let him convince me to relocate there with him. He told me that he now had an excellent job and begged me to join him. He said that he had changed and that things would be different and that we would be a family. I believed him, and I believed in us, so I went.

My daughter and I moved to Washington DC to start our new lives. I got a job, enrolled my daughter in kindergarten. He had family there, so we stayed with them for a while until we found a place of our own. But things took a turn for the worse and MC began to assault me once again. It was to the point where I began to fight back, and things became very violent. We began to break items in the house such as lamps, tables, chairs, etc. There was a time that he even choked me until I lost consciousness. At that point, I knew that he was really "crazy,

He also began to spy on me because there were times when I thought he was at work, and he would be outside of our home hiding in the bushes, spying on me. Although I was not doing anything wrong, he would say things like "I saw you with the mailman." He was so controlling and manipulative, but the fear had already been instilled in me, so I felt like I was stuck and could not go anywhere or do anything.

At some point, I began to plot my escape because I knew in my heart that I could no longer live like this. I could not do this anymore. I was tired. My daughter saw what was happening, and I needed to protect her. I knew that I could not tell him that I was planning to leave him or else he would hurt me more. When he put his gun to my head, I knew that he could possibly kill me one day.

I began to save money from the part time job that I was working. My neighbor was in on the plan. She would allow me to hide clothes and my suitcases at her house. Once I had enough money saved I bought a one-way greyhound bus ticket to go back home to my family, and I only had to plan it out the right way.

The day had finally come for me to be free. MC went to work. As soon as I thought that he was gone, I called a cab and me and my daughter went to the bus station, hopped on that bus and began our long journey back home.

When I got back to home, I stayed with a family member for a while until I was able to get my own place. Meanwhile, MC moved back home as well. He somehow was able to get in touch with me. He came to my house so that we could talk. He said he was a changed man and that he wanted to have a fresh start. I told him "No!" and demanded that he leave my house. He did not like my demeanor and began to choke me and then slammed me on the floor. My neighbors heard what was going on and called the police. The police made him leave. I later filed a report and had him put in jail.

This man was so crazy that when he got out of jail, he came to my house late at night. Ringing my doorbell for me to let him in. I had a chain lock on the door, so I am slowly opening the door with the chain lock on. He was standing there saying, please let me in so we can talk. He then tried to force his way in. I slammed the door so hard on his foot that I thought I broke it. I let him know that my brother and male cousins were looking for him and could perhaps harm him if he bothered me again.

After that, I got a new telephone number, and I told his mom to talk to her son because if he kept harassing me that I was going to make sure that he did time in jail. I wasn't afraid anymore, and I was ready, willing and able to fight back. He finally understood the depth of my emotions and left me alone.

You see, for a very long time I was verbally, mentally, sexually, and physically abused by this man. There were times when he was asleep that I wanted to cause harm to him. Make him hurt like I hurt. But the God in me couldn't do it. I made it out of one of the worst abusive relationships that one could endure.

There are so many other violent acts that I could share in this story, but they are still too painful for me to write about. I may have been bruised, but I'm not broken. I am stronger and wiser and in one of the best relationships, I have ever been in with my Heavenly Father. And because of this, No one, I mean no one, can ever come between my Heavenly Father and me. I am the Queen of my castle and my life.

I say to each of you reading this story, I am Still Standing through it all and I am a survivor. I survived so that I can share my story with you to bring a sense of understanding and healing to your life.

Please, never let anyone hit you, curse you, or control you because that is not love. Love is patient, and Love is Kind.

I have listed the warning signs of abuse on the next page. Please pay attention to the signs and red flags. And don't be afraid to ask for help.

# Survival Talk...

# Identify various forms of abuse

There are many forms of Domestic Abuse; some of which we tend to overlook for various reasons such as love, compassion, marital/relationship arrangement, financial dependency, or childhood past. These hurtful, harmful acts cause wounding in our lives— ultimately bringing us to a place of confusion, brokenness or shame.

The first step is clearly identifying abuse.

**Physical Abuse**
Shoving, hitting, pulling, choking, biting, kicking, abandoning, isolation, head-butting, pinching, slapping, throwing things.

**Verbal Abuse**
Name calling, insulting, threatening, demeaning, raising tone of voice, profane verbal outburst.

**Emotional Abuse**
Ignoring, threatening, intimating, using traumatic situations or experiences against you, threating to harm themselves, threating to harm children, friends or family members.

**Financial/Economic Abuse**

Financially controlling, Stealing from bank/credit card accounts, denial of financial resources, intentional damage to credit, withholding support for children.

**Sexual Abuse**

Sex by force. Sex without mutual consent.

## Chapter Two

## A PLAN FOR YOUR LIFE
By Bernadine C. Taylor

Even if you have never been a victim of domestic violence, there is still a lot to learn from a "*Survivor...*" You must have a "plan for your life." And not only a plan for your life; but a plan for your children's life, and plan for your "*peace.*" A purpose without a plan is powerless, which is why......

The thought never crossed my mind that I would be snatched suddenly out of bed at approximately three o'clock a.m. on a Sunday morning to the words.... "Get up *blank blank blank*, we gon' fight tonight!" Pregnant body and all jolted into action to a stance I could not quite balance out of fear that my legs would slip from beneath me when I was pulled up by my arm. I tried to cuff my huge stomach with my other hand and silently prayed that this was *my husband* on the prowl, and not just some random intruder. I tried to gain my composure and snap out of sleep into *consciousness* while at the same time try to be brave as I worried that my other *two* small children were okay, as this *could still* be a home invasion of some sort.

Based on the recent chain of events, coupled with the unusual traffic, in particular; crooked cops, guns, rifles, police scanners, busted car windows as bricks are thrown into them, you name it, amid my husband's many explicit escapades, losing friends to "witness protection"; no no no this certainly wasn't the first scare.

The last straw, however, was when his *main man* was shot and killed, and he ran home to whisk the children and me off to my sister's house, not knowing what had transpired. This was the same *main man* that I protested, some years earlier, that I didn't want to be in my wedding as the *best man*.

"Why not?" my husband retorted.

"Because, I don't want my bridal party or my guest being shot up!"

"Awl, girl, ain't nuttin' like dat, gonna happen…"

That was my point, needless to say, he passed before the wedding, and my husband was crushed, all he could muster up was "*That was supposed to be my best man.*"

I started to do what I was beginning to become more and more accustomed to doing, and that was *'ignore him.'* Mario blasted the music so loud as we drove to the funeral; I yelled, "turn that music down! Have some respect for the dead."

"Dis not even loud!"

"Yes, It is!"

"No, it's not!"

"Well, it's not gospel music!"

"You and your *gospel* music….dis *Bobby Brown, it's my prerogative…I do what I wanna do…*"

Singing and bopping his head up and down until his Mother finally agreed and encouraged him to turn it down. I was more than happy for her to drive in the front seat with him… In my mind, she was *Cissy Houston,* and I was *Whitney,* but he was *her* son. People would say to me… *"You two are just as different as night and day."* Clearly I ignored naysayers at the time. I wanted the institution of "family" and I was spent on trying to salvage my marriage.

Needless to say, the voice in my daughter's dark bedroom became more familiar as I shook the grogginess off. I was thrilled that I just so happened to have fallen asleep with *Rachael in her bed,* since my husband didn't know how to come home at night, or at least at a decent hour, to read our five-year-old a bedtime story or to even say goodnight to us. Mario, Jr., was a mere two.

I cannot phantom why I was surprised since I had to take a cab to the hospital when I was in labor with our oldest child because he came and took the car in the middle of the night…. You often hear people say *"signs everywhere."* Then for the thirteen hours of labor, there he snored in the rocking chair, at 4 a.m. (after he arrived) while his mother and sister squeezed my hand with every sharp contraction.

But after many years of disappointing the children and my tiring of making up excuses as to where their father was at dinnertime,

26

my psyche could only think of one thing, *no two things*, first to begin to eat dinner without him, and then *two*, stop saving a plate wrapped in foil on the stove.

Mind still racing, I surmised no way could this be an intruder. *"Not in this neighborhood."* Nobody had *"nothing."* We only had remote controls for the television, no internet, like today, thank goodness or *Facebook*. We didn't have to put our business on the street... We did our own *"detective"* work. Whether I knew or not where the car was parked, the town was so small, you could just run into your spouse at a nightclub, or some girlfriend will tell you where the car was. I'd often just trade cars, or take the car altogether; so when Mario would come out of his Mistresses' house in the wee hours of the morning. There would be no car to jump into.

The latest car was my brand new black Chevy Corsica that during the heated divorce battle, Mario lurked behind my house while I escorted my baby sister out, and snatched the keys out of my hand, and had the audacity to call upset that I cancelled the *"disability"* insurance, when I was the one that had to go out sick on disability, *not him*! In part, due to his infidelity, I became ill and nearly miscarried four months in. I thought for sure; I was going to lose our third baby because of the *STD* he gave me while doing and sleeping around with who knows *"what."* I had been complaining of excruciating pain. The doctor detected the infection and prescribed medication right away and told me to get tested.

At any rate, I quickly gather my senses as good as anyone could under the circumstances and took a wild guess, a good as a peek as I could, and as rough of a nudge as I tried and shouted his name... "MARIO TATE!...... What is wrong with you?!...You should have stayed gone and fought them dudes on the street where you just came from instead of coming in here dragging me out of bed tryna fight me! You crazy?!"

"I might be crazy cuz I just lost all my money shootin' crap."

"Crap, are you serious, crap yo' a#* on outta here before you wake the children up!"

"I don't care! Dis my house! I wake up whoever I want!"

He stomped off... I tightened my robe, huffed and puffed, and can't go back to sleep. Actually *scared* to go back to sleep. So I went to the bathroom, tiptoed to check on the children, thanked the *Father* above that they didn't wake up with all his commotion.

You quickly learn how to walk lightly when you're dealing with an abuser, as they can strike at any time. The slightest noise can tick them off. And although you proceed with *discretion advised,* you tend to look at the current upheavals as another episode, not *abuse,* which makes it difficult to leave at times.

Generally, by no fault of your own, there's a totally different mindset going on. One that you're not even aware of, particularly if you grew up and/or was raised in an abusive environment. But always follow your heart, as it will never lie to you because abuse rears its ugly head in many different forms rather it be *physical, mental, verbal or sexual* and it can take quite an *emotional* toll on your heart and mind.

With that being said, and at a brassy twenty-three, I followed my *poor little naïve sweetheart* and instead of lying back down, my quiet steps led me to the unfathomable... watching my husband, sitting at our kitchen table, with a syringe wrapped around a propped elbow with a needle about to land on his arm...

"Mario... stop it! What are you doing??!!"

"Get out of here, woman..." fanning his hand for me to scurry off while trying to hover over the tiny "*I dream of Jeannie*" glass type bottle.

How did I go from "girl to woman" within the same hour, I will never know, but that's not strange; he'd began to start calling me his *mistress'* name for heaven's sake... But the feeling that I felt walking away eluded me to the fact that he needed help, or I may not get out of the house alive. He was now way beyond smoking and drinking, and I was determined not to be dragged down into the gutter with him (*Nope! not a part of my plan*).

Every time Mario would slap or punch me, I would pick up my children, and drive off to one of my sister's houses. My one sister would kindly open her door, even though I could tell she didn't want to; here I was, two children, black eyes, busted lips, toothless sigh… she was becoming weary just as I; with my constant going back….

"But Nay Nay, This is my husband."

"And husband's promise to love and cherish not beat you."

"He was high."

That was me making excuses. DON'T! Once he told me that my father messed up for *him* because I wasn't about to let him live like my father did (who had three mistresses and a wife and fifteen children between them). I had *a plan for my life* before I met my husband.

As a child, I saw the result of my mother being beaten for "no reason." Hiding us from the pain. So the next words finally resonated with me spoken by one of my oldest sisters… I always looked up to her because Nay Nay was humble and real, an awesome caregiver and not to mention an excellent cook. Til this day, she may not know that the words she spoke helped me to overcome and put my *plan* for *my* life into action. I was always a woman of deep faith, and there were numerous times that I would just hold the Bible to my chest and pray and also use it to ward off Mario's attacks. *"Jump back Jack,"*… with both arms extended in front of his face, *"Don't you come any closer."* He was spooked by it. When in danger, my philosophy was, *whatever works.*

So my sister calmly admonished…. *"When you get tired, you gon' leave, let's just pray it's not too late… Now, what's your plan for tomorrow… are you leaving for good this time?!"*

Especially since I would show up at family gatherings and church with black eyes, just so if anyone wanted to talk about me, they could (in front of my face) or ask any questions. I was there to defend myself, and my children. Silly pride. But I was not ashamed about something I allowed. I would put makeup on to cover up my bruises. I even felt I was becoming stronger because I started to take pictures so that I could have my own proof in Court… I was definitely going to get a divorce. I could not subject my two children and then one on the way to such inhumane treatment.

So, I walked back down the hall to try to block out the scene; only to be grabbed from the behind. I screamed out the children's names out of panic; I had to wake them….

"Get up, come now, your daddy is trying to kill me!!"

He made them go back to their rooms, pushed me into another room, slung me around and pointed a butcher knife at my belly.

As if they could ward their Dad, off, in an instant, both children charged into the room. Each one wrapped their arms around each one of his legs, crying and hitting, *"leave Mommy alone."* He pushed the children off his legs. Now I'm crushed because it's one thing to fight me, but now pushing my babies down, I cannot bear.

I didn't want to turn my back again, as there was a window and I didn't want to go through it... didn't want to step forward because this was a big blade (and I instantly recalled the last time a butcher knife was involved... I had grabbed it to stab him, and he snatched it back, so I snatched my oldest daughter and jumped down a whole flight of stairs and never stopped running until I came upon the neighborhood police station)... so I was not about to relive that.... So I did all that *I could do*.... I STOOD STILL....

Then after a few moments, I finally spoke...

"So this is what you're going to do? Take me out like this? C'mon then, "do it, do it, Mario!"

I called his bluff when I saw him look down. I immediately grabbed what I had tucked *"in sight"* *a baseball bat*, I began to bang his feet with it just to distract him, so I could open the back door and run out of it for help. No cells phones, mind you, we still had pay phones, *working pay phones at that*, at every corner.

But this night, in particular, I just swallowed my pride and ran to a neighbor's house. The first neighbor refused to help me; the second neighbor turned off the porch light, but the third neighbor let me in and called the police, and asked where the children were and a whole bunch of other questions.

32

*"I left them in the house with him. I couldn't grab them this time, it's two of them now,* and I patted my belly, another on the way."

She shook her head in dismay. I was so ashamed. Shame coupled with fear, means at times, a good recipe for *makeup*, as the abuser is the only one *who you think* really loves you. You are not looking at the *"didn't he just beat me"* sign. And don't let a family emergency arise, like death or murder; *if you're not careful*, for your abuser to weasel back into your heart.

The police came, and I met them at the house, but before I knew it, they put me in the car, reading me my rights, with a shove on the head to put me in the back seat. "Whaat?! Why am I being arrested?" He attacked me, and he has my children!"

"Get in the car 'Mam!" I forgot Mario had all these friends on the force. I'm baffled because one is a "Brotha'."

Now something is wrong with this picture; I fumed. Mario was at his old tricks again. He had told the cops that I attacked him with a baseball bat. He was on the phone with his mother; crying (literally) that he didn't do a thing to me coupled with the fact that he had each child resting comfortably on his knees.

Today's generation would say, *"smh"* – and that's what I was doing, all the way to the Precinct! A lineup, a pat down, a mug shot… what kind of stuff is this! Men mumbled, *"wonder what she is doing here?"* another *"looks like her old man beat her up."* I looked up at the men, with that, *"I can hear you"* look!

33

Everything after that was a blur. How I got out, who came and got me, where my children were, where was I going? My first phone call.

In lock up, I heard officers marching through the hall, scathing their police sticks along the bars, making that clanging sound, and then I hear "Tate?! "Let's go!" Naturally, I followed suit. My sisters came and got me. Mario, who didn't want to be bothered anyway with the children, called Nay Nay and had her pick them up. Once I made it to her house; she let me peek in on them so I can see they were safe and sound and as we would say back in the day, *"sleeping as good as a bug in a rug."*

The next morning, I knew what I had to do. LEAVE! I was infuriated, humiliated, and to say the least, finally TIRED. My sister's words rehearsed in my head, over and over again, *"when you get tired, you will leave."* But this was not about me leaving, "Oh no, when I woke up the next morning, I assured my sister, "I am NOT LEAVING." She was in shock. Surely that was the last straw, and in the words of my mother, "that broke the camel's back!" Indeed, it was! I told my sisters "Wait, I am not leaving. I said it right. No, no no. He's leaving!!!"

That's all they needed to hear. You would have thought we were in the Army. Fully invigorated we put the plan into action. My sister's friend had a van. We drove to my house and gathered up all of Mario's belongings and put everything we could into those large green "Glad" (for more than one reason) garbage bags. Nay stopped short of pulling off from the house and said, "WAIT! He cannot come back and he will because he has keys so what I am going to do, right now, is change the locks!"

"We don't have that kind of time to go buy locks or money."

"Don't you worry!"

My sister jumped out the van, went back into the house, grabbed a screwdriver and said, "watch this!"

She started unscrewing her locks from her door and talking at the same time, "we will just exchange locks. I'll put these on your house, and take yours off and put them on mine."

Meanwhile, I notice my funny sister *Cora* doing some fist fighting moves on the sidewalk, making "woofing sounds."

"Woof woof."

"What are you doing?"

"The Cassius Clay…"

"The who?"

"The Cassius Clay" throwing jabs, shifting her feet back and forth, "yea, yea, you know him… *Muhammed Ali*, you know his name use to be *Cassius Clay* before it was *Muhammed Ali,* and that's what umma do to Mario when I see him. You might be scared of him, but I ain't!"

My first laugh in I don't know how long. All I could do is watch all of this unfold and to see how creative and bold my sisters were being in helping to deliver me out of this misery. It was long overdue. And I was nearly due beginning my ninth month of pregnancy. My sister Ann stayed behind to watch all of our children. So here we were back at my house. I had already got rid of his best friend. Our dog. (When Mario stayed gone for days at a time and would finally come home, the dog would bark at him).

My one sister tossed bags in the van while NayNay replaced the locks. Once everything was packed up, Cora, said, "alright, let's go. Where his mother live because that's where all this stuff is going."

"Well, we can't just show up can we?"

"Why not? This is it! It's over. We are showing up! If he not there, then we will set all his belongings on his mother's front lawn!"

Busiest street in the small, tight-knit community is where we landed. I was told to stay in the van. Cora jumped out and knocked on the door.

"Is Mario here?"

His brother answered, "wait here…"

You don't mess with this sister. She was the female version of "*Dennis-the-Menace*" we called her growing up. She didn't wait at the door but immediately went and opened up the side door of the van. It was one of those old ones where you see the tire and a ladder on the back of it. Burgandy. With those funny square windows and blinds. There I was peering out as Cora began to throw bags upon bags on the lawn. Mario comes to the door in a rage...

"What you doing?!"

"What it look like!" my sister boldly responded. Then from nowhere she yells "Do something, you feel froggish leap!"

Mario goes to swing at her. She slides out of the way and runs into the middle of the street and taunts him "C'mon... um ready..."

She kicks her shoes off. Lo and behold, Mario kicks his shoes off. I am in amazement. Shocked that he is really going to engage. Cars are stopping. It is quite a sight. His mother and brothers and sisters are yelling, "Y'all stop!"

My sister hollered some profanities and kept swinging at him, just like she practiced, got some blows in too. Mario couldn't get any what we called "*licks*" in because he was being pulled to and fro.

Cora continued to taunt "unt-un, let him go! Offering expletives. He wants to fight my sister. Naw, naw. Fight me!"

He noticed me in the van and tried to run towards the door. My sister chased him and stopped him. Slung him out of the way.

She slammed the doors and jumped in, and Nay Nay screeched off. Leaving Mario in the street yelling. I thought I was going to have the baby that day from laughter.

A week later, I received DIVORCE papers. FINALLY FREE! I remember meeting with the Attorney, who stated, *"He may have you beat by fist but you have him beat by brains."*

# Survival Talk...

## Have a Survival Plan

— Your life depends on it!

Plan A

Plan B

Plan C

Plan D

Help !

If you are currently experiencing acts of Domestic Abuse, it is important to find resources that can help you plan to leave the situation.

*Think before you react.

* During an argument try your best to stay calm. Try to avoid arguing in rooms such as the kitchen which has sharp objects or rooms that only have one way in and out like the bathroom.

*Identify a safe place (a friend's house that your mate would not look to find you or hotel (if close to your home, be sure to have the phone number to the hotel security easily accessible).

*Always keep a telephone cell phone, or internet connection capabilities readily available at ALL times. Program your equipment using its voice feature to identify an emergency tone within your voice. Example: Speaking into your device say the following... "Help" or use a 'CODE WORD" so that your phone, tablet or other programmable device calls for help if you are in a stressful situation. Code words are also good to have to alert children, friends or family members if you find yourself in a position of distress when you're dealing with an abusive partner.

*Be cautious and safe.

*Build a support system.

*Identify at least one-two to confide in will be of support when you decide to leave.

*Inform your child's school administrator/childcare provider that your family will be in transition due to an abusive partner. Also noting that potential absences may occur during your transition period so that they are aware. Sometimes they too may be able to offer various alternatives and resources to help.

*Check your company's FMLA/Family Violence Leave Policy for details of terms and compensation information to know rights as well as your benefits, should you need to take time off of work.

*Always keep money, important papers and documentation with you at all times.

*Strategically pack clothing in an inconspicuous, yet easily accessible location; so that your partner does not suspect your plan. (This may cause your partner to become frustrated and abusive).

*Learn the route to your safe destination and plan a transportation method if you do not own a car. Always be sure to have access tools like keys or keyless entry devices to vehicle handy.

*Get a Post Office Box in an easy access area that will not reveal your safe place to begin forwarding your mail correspondences.

Sometimes you may not be in a position to plan, therefore in all emergency situations its best to call your local authorities or 911 for assistance.

# Chapter Three

## FROM TRIAL TO TRIUMPH: DATING THE ENEMY
By Dr. Catrina Pullum

Do not return evil for evil or insult for insult, but give a blessing instead; for you were called for the very purpose that you might inherit a blessing. 1 Peter 3:9

While in preparation for my senior year in college, I met the man of my dreams "my prince charming." My prince charming was handsome, polite, and said all of the right things. He was a gentleman and a family man who wined and dined me. He came at a very vulnerable time in my life when I had already gone through several trials, so he indeed was in my mind, a Godsend. He not only showed interest in me but also in getting to know my son, but I couldn't understand why my son refused to get to know him. The first two months of our relationship was awesome. He asked me to move in with him, and I did because I was "in love." I was so in love that I did not see how my son was feeling about him, nor did I pick up on the signs of how my son was reacting to my relationship.

Two days after meeting my beau, I was asked to meet his family who were very influential in the community. Everything seemed so perfect and on the surface appeared to exceed my expectations. A few days later, I received a call from his sister warning me to be careful because my beau, her brother was an abuser and had been abusive to his ex-wife. I confronted my beau who denied the claims (not that I expected anything else), and I believed him. He stated that his sister was lying on him because she did not like him and that his mother had been physically abusive toward him while he was growing up. He stated that he had a love-hate relationship with his mother because she used to beat him on his hands with spoons. The fact that he was distant from the females in his family didn't send up any red flags for me at the time because I simply believed in who he presented to be.

A few weeks later, I noticed a change in his behavior, and this is where my domestic violence journey began, in the summer of 1997-the longest 8-month journey of my life. This is where the representation of him the reflection of a man that I fell in love with fell off the face of the earth, and his "true personality" emerged. It started out really    subtle; he  would tell me where I could and could not go and who I could and could not talk to. He began making spontaneous and unannounced visits to the college campus where I was attending, verifying  that I was in attendance in my classes as well as questioning the times I would be home. I attempted to seek help by verbalizing to our families about his behaviors. However, he was so charming in the presence of others, that everyone felt that I was lying about his actions except for his family. He was very obsessive about his military career and pleasing his father.

One evening while driving to the mall, one of my fraternity brothers blew his horn at me as a gesture of speaking. My Enemy abruptly ordered that I change directions, turn around and go home. Upon entering the apartment, he proceeded to punch a hole in the wall and pushed me in the bedroom. While in the bedroom, he raped and choked me, all while accusing me of cheating on him. All of this was prompted by a simple wave from my fraternity brother. Once he calmed down, he told me that it was my fault and that my behavior was the reason for his actions, the normal spill of an abuser.

A week after the initial attack, my great-grandmother, who had been sick for some time, illness progressed and landed her in the hospital in ICU. It was a no-brainer for me, I had to go and see her because she was not only my great-grandmother but a mother to me, because she was the one who raised me. Instead of just allowing me to visit my great-grandmother, he gave me an ultimatum; it was either her or him. Needless to say, I chose to go see her because I didn't know how much longer she had to live. I also feared that I would feel his wrath when I returned home and I did. I received a beating upon returning home. My grandmother passed away the next day, and my family called for me to come to the hospital. He was reluctant to bring me but did. When I made it to my family, they notified me that I would have to make arrangements for the funeral out of town where my grandmother lived. This meant "we" would be leaving town for a week, or so I thought. He not only refused to attend with me, but also refused to address some of my attempts to talk to him about it...our conversations were limited. He was angry, stating that I abandoned him by not being home to cook for him and making sure that he was taken care of. When I returned home, I received another beating. From that day on, I was randomly beaten at least four times a week, sometimes for his "justifiable" reasons while other times for no reason at all. There were times I was beaten while my son watched and other times he wasn't present. This made my son apprehensive of being in my ex's presence, and my son would refuse to stay in the home with my ex when I had to leave. He received the most pleasure in choking me, once telling me that it gave him a rush.

Although I was in school full-time, I had been caring for my great-grandmother. She was the person who raised me from the age of two months old, so she was the one I called mother. Her health was deteriorating rapidly and, in addition, I was still caring for my five-year-old son. I was also serving as the president of my sorority, member of SGA, and a member of various other organizations. I was very family oriented and a socialite up until this point. During this period, I had very limited contact with my family and friends. I was only allowed to go to school and work. I could not attend any functions without him. In front of my family and friends, he would act if he loved me so much yet while we were alone, The Enemy would return. Over the course of the relationship, I began to notice a decline in my son's behavior in which he began to display anger in violent ways.

In March of 1998, my professors suspected something was going wrong in my life due to my excessive absences from class, missed assignments, etc. which was a significant change from my previous situation. Before Dating The Enemy, I was an outgoing and focused student, dedicated to my education, and excelling in every facet. My grades were failing, and my smile was no longer there. I was skipping class and not turning in assignments to my professors. It finally hit me when I received my failing progress report and after seeing the fear on my son's face, "It was time to leave" and I did. This is the day I took a stand knowing God had my back. I looked up and prayed to God that if HE got me out of that situation that I would not return. I looked to The Enemy to say that I was leaving. He stated that it was fine, "Go" but as I proceeded to I walk away, he placed a butcher knife to my throat. At this point, I was no longer intimidated by him, or what he could do to me, I was ready to go. I stood up to him and reminded him that I worked for law enforcement and that if he'd made the decision to kill me that the FBI would spare no expense in a search for him. He dropped the knife and left the apartment.

I called the first person I could think of ….momma!! I explained the horror that I had been living; she then advised me that if she was in my shoes that she would leave. She stated that it was my choice to make and that she would support me no matter what choice I made. That day was the day that I left and moved back home.

I filed criminal charges against him along with a restraining order. My restraining order was granted, and he was arrested. He attempted to persuade my maternal grandparents to convince me to drop the charges. My grandmother initially sided with him, convinced that he was truly the nice guy he presented himself to be. She would say, "there is no way he did all of those things." I refused to drop the charges, which caused a strain in the relationship that my grandmother and I shared. It strained our relationship to a point that over a 2-year span, we didn't communicate at all. His family, although they knew the type of violent man he was and his history of being an abuser, was also upset that I pressed charges against him. The notable exception was his father, with whom I maintained a relationship with until I relocated. My case progressed very slowly through the justice system, because sometimes The Enemy would show up and sometimes he would not. He claimed that he could not find attorney representation, true or not; I did not know or care. After several court appearances with no progress over a period of 6 months, I decided to drop the case and move away for a fresh start.

Two years later, I received a call from my grandmother apologizing for not believing in me. She stated that agents from the FBI were looking for me after reviewing my case against my ex. They wanted to notify me that they had arrested him for a murder that he had committed in a previous domestic violence case before dating me. They stated that he had a history of violence towards women. At that moment, I felt a release of fear.

Why did I stay you ask?? I stayed because I did not want to feel like a failure. I stayed for eight months and endured physical, emotional and verbal abuse along with rape. I was made aware of services that are available to survivors when I filed criminal charges, yet I chose to counsel myself. For a long time, I have suppressed things and lived in fear of being hurt, not realizing this was the source of my anger and fear until I began to process my situation. My son also received years of therapy to manage his anger and his behavior. He says that he does not remember what happened, that he only recalls not liking him. He is a productive member of society today. He is a college student and business owner.

As for me, today I am a successful Entrepreneur, Wife, and Mother. I am still at times guarded but have zero tolerance for violence. There are times that I flash back to what happened to me, but I continue to pray daily that God keeps me covered. My release is when I can help young women who presently are where God's delivered me from. Through the sharing of my story with everyone, I proclaim, "This is your time for healing". I could have been murder victim number 2 of my ex, but God had a different plan for me. I am a survivor, and I am living to share my testimony.

Those 8 months in 1997 were truly a trial! But remember, God uses our trials to draw us closer to Him, increase our reliance upon Him, and to bring us ultimately into our triumph! I thank God that I was able to truly move from Trial to Triumph! I hope my story enables others to do the same. I'll leave you with a scripture that I hold near and dear, and that helped me to make it through such a tumultuous time in my life: Psalm 91 which reads:

## Psalm 91

<sup>1</sup> Whoever dwells in the shelter of the Most High
  will rest in the shadow of the Almighty
<sup>2</sup> I will say of the LORD, "He is my refuge and my fortress,
  my God, in whom I trust."

<sup>3</sup> Surely he will save you
  from the fowler's snare
  and from the deadly pestilence.
<sup>4</sup> He will cover you with his feathers,
  and under his wings you will find refuge;
  his faithfulness will be your shield and rampart.
<sup>5</sup> You will not fear the terror of night,
  nor the arrow that flies by day,
<sup>6</sup> nor the pestilence that stalks in the darkness,
  nor the plague that destroys at midday.
<sup>7</sup> A thousand may fall at your side,
  ten thousand at your right hand,
  but it will not come near you.
<sup>8</sup> You will only observe with your eyes
  and see the punishment of the wicked.

<sup>9</sup> If you say, "The LORD is my refuge,"
  and you make the Most High your dwelling,
<sup>10</sup> no harm will overtake you,
  no disaster will come near your tent.
<sup>11</sup> For he will command his angels concerning you
  to guard you in all your ways;
<sup>12</sup> they will lift you up in their hands,
  so that you will not strike your foot against a stone.

¹³ You will tread on the lion and the cobra;
   you will trample the great lion and the serpent.

¹⁴ "Because he[b] loves me," says the LORD, "I will rescue him;
   I will protect him, for he acknowledges my name.
¹⁵ He will call on me, and I will answer him;
   I will be with him in trouble;
   I will deliver him and honor him.
¹⁶ With long life, I will satisfy him
   and show him my salvation."

# Survival Talk...

## Feeling Free

Freedom: The quality or state of being free: as

The absence of necessity, coercion, or constraint in choice or action.

Liberation from slavery or restraint or from the power of another: Independence

The quality or state of being exempt or released usually from something onerous

The quality of being frank, open or outspoken

Boldness

What makes you feel free?

What makes you feel controlled?

Do you have a feeling of rebellion when you feel that you want to be free?

# Chapter Four

## SILENT NO MORE
By Sharon Willingham

"We know that all things (good and bad) work together for the good

to them that love the Lord and who are called according to his

purpose!" (Romans 8:28, emphasis mine)

On average, more than three women a day are murdered by the hands of their husbands or boyfriends in the United States. In 2005, 1,181 women were murdered. Nearly one in four women in the United States has reported experiencing violence by a current or former spouse or boyfriend at some point in their lives. I was one of those women. I have survived to tell my story and break the silence. I have hidden my suffering of abuse for many years until now. (CDC Center for Disease Control Prevent 2008 Published).

We dated for two years before getting married. We met each other through a mutual friend. He was a handsome, intelligent, small business owner. We were in love with each other. We were inseparable. He decided to join the Army to further his career. I stayed behind to continue working and to take care of my niece. We talked to each on the phone just about every night. Our relationship was solid. I was in love with Victor and we planned to get married after he finished training and was assigned to a permanent duty station in North Carolina. I eventually moved there to be with him, and thrilled about the idea of us finally being together. Shortly after my arrival to North Carolina, the lies started. He told me that he had an apartment for us to live in, but to my surprise, that was a lie. There was no apartment. We had to stay at his friends house, which really upset me. But he was able to smooth things over with his charm and said, "I will make it up to you." I believed him.

Everything seemed to be going great. He was loving, devoted, extremely smart, and focused on succeeding in his career in the Army. He was my friend, my confidant, and my protector. He treated me like a queen. My husband was kind and generous to friends, family, and strangers. I never suspected that Victor could have a violent rage in him. It did not show until the day he tried to strangle me to death.

The abuse began in 1987, months after we were married. We were talking in the parking lot of my job at Sears during my lunch break. I questioned him about what I learned of his possible cheating. He denied it and became very angry. Out of nowhere, he grabbed me by my neck and began to strangle me. Someone witnessed what was happening and called the Army police. The officer showed up and asked me if I wanted to file a complaint and press charges against him. I was still in shock! Victor said to me," If you press charges, I will get thrown out of the Army." I felt that it was my fault and that he would lose his job. I felt sorry for him, so I didn't file a complaint nor did I press charges. I did not tell anyone about what he did to me. He apologized eventually and said, "I did not mean to hurt you. I will never put my hands on you again." That was the day that he gained control over me. That was the day the abusive cycle began. Later, I found out he lied about the cheating; it was true.

I felt that perhaps I could change some of his behavior by showing him love and spending time with him as a way to let him know that I wanted to make our marriage work. But that didn't work. The verbal abuse and controlling ways became very intense. He refused to help me with transportation as means of control, and he continuoulsly messed with my mind and my emotions. I decided I was going to leave him and go back to New Jersey with my family, but found out that I was pregnant. I was extremely happy, but he was not there for me. During this time my sister, Tonya came down to live with us to finish her last year of High school.

She revealed to me he was having an affair. I was so furious that I went into a rage. I found out where his mistress lived and went to her house. His car was parked outside, and he refused to come out of the house. Once we were able to discuss it, he denied everything and made up stories. I continued to stay with him even after he denied the affair. Once I had my son, I thought our relationship would grow closer, but he still continued to be unstable.

He decided that he no longer wanted to stay in the Army, so we eventually moved back to New Jersey. Once we were back in New Jersey, he had no stable employment, so we lost everything. The car was repossessed, the house was in foreclosure, and to add to this devastation, I was pregnant with our second child. He finally found a job. While working, he had another affair with one of his co-workers. When I found out, I confrtonted him. Of course, he denied it. He became so angry and tried to strangle me while I was on the sofa. I fought and begged for my life that day. Thankfully, I was able to get away, and he was arrested for assault. I became so distraught that I went into a state of depression. I did not want to live anymore, but God spoke to me. He said, "I will never leave you nor forsake you." God said that He loved me and that my children were a blessing from Him; and that they needed me. After God had spoken to me, I left the house and moved to another state. Over a period of time, we eventually we got back together. He made a promise to me to not be abusive, cheat or use drugs again.

Well, that promise was broken. He started using drugs at a terrifying rate. Only now, the hallucinations had begun. He sometimes sat up all night looking out the window thinking he saw snipers in the trees waiting to attack the house. He also began a pattern of unstable employment. The cycle began again. The severity of rage increased with time, as did his drug abuse. I had come to believe that the drugs were not the cause of his violence. He was always prone to having a violent and controlling nature. The drugs did make the mood swings more sudden and more severe. I got through that period of my life through the grace of God.

All of a suddern one day, he came home and said, "I just re-dedicated my life back to Christ." I, too, re-dedicated my life back to the Lord in 1994. We both felt the Lord was calling us back to live in New Jersey, so we moved once again.

After all the years that we were married, Victor decides he wants to become jealous. It became increasingly apparent that he wanted my attention at all times. I was at his beck and call. I cooked, cleaned, and served him. But that didn't matter. My husband seemed to have more pent up anger as the years went on. I started to feel like I was always walking on eggshells around him. When I would try to discuss anything about how I felt, he would get agitated and turn it into an argument. I soon realized it was easier just to appease him to keep the peace. I noticed the kids' demeanor changed as well as my own when my husband would arrive home because we never knew what type of mood he would be in. Sometimes, he would snap for no reason.

Many times, after being abusive, my husband would seem remorseful for physically, emotionally, and verbally abusing me. He would buy me things as a sign of being apologetic. However, as the abuse became more frequent and more torture-like in nature, as if he seemed to enjoy the pain and suffering he inflicted on me. I felt so alone and isolated but knew I couldn't leave or tell anyone. From the outside looking in, we had it all, but what was missing was my sense of peace and personal safety.

During this time period, God had blessed me with a hair salon that was very successful. Financially, we were doing well. As years went on, the situation grew worse. He started using drugs again. At this point, the drug use escalated and he was unstable with employment yet again. His episodes of extreme rage towards me became increasingly frequent. He was often lazy and selfish when it came to doing chores and helping around the house. He began entertaining young women claiming he was their counselor because they didn't have a father figure. He used this as an excuse to justify the affairs which I later found out about.

I told him on many occasions that it was inappropriate, but he became angrier when I questioned his judgment. Victor had the audacity to claim he was ministering to them. He was having affairs with the young women he was so-called counseling for years. First he denied, and eventually he confessed but did not stop. He would pick arguments so I could put him out of the house to justify the affairs. To make matter worse, while on my computer one day, I discovered he was surfing the web for pornography. The more and more he watched adult movies and websites, the more he started acting out the fantasies of them on me. On some occasions, I didn't even want to have sex because he was so aggressive.

Everyone thought of us as "the perfect family." To keep the peace, I hid his drug habits, his affairs, and the abuse from my friends, my family, and his family. Although he had this horrible side, he was a remarkable father and person at times. He had become a Dr. Jekyll and Mr. Hyde; it would come and go. Time after time, he would apologize and promise that it would never happen again. I would hope that maybe, this time would be different. Occasionally, he was the master of psychological manipulation. He loved to play games. When I would do something to displease him, he would ask about the incident in such a way as to make any answer seem extraordinarily out of pocket. The questions were almost rhetorical; yet, he always demanded an answer. My non-response infuriated him even more, usually resulting in aggressive verbal abuse or a threatening act. Victor often played these games with the children and me in slightly different forms tailored to our reactions.

His control over me was increasing. He used threats and intimidation. When he felt he needed to take strong measures, he would grab me tightly or grab me by my neck. The amount of times that he would snap and go into a physically violent rage were actually rare compared to what one might imagine. They occurred on the average of once every other month, although sometimes, more or less frequently.

He once tried to impersonate a police officer and was arrested which resulted in him losing his job with the federal government. This time, he was on a tyrannical rampage. The police were called, and he was arrested and charged with domestic assault. He was convicted of the offense, placed on one-year probation, and mandated by the court to attend a Men's Domestic Violence Program. Somehow he managed to get by not having to complete the program. He lost his job because of his behavior, but blamed me for everything that was happening to him. Our financial situation was deteriorating, and I was very stressed out. He started to humiliate me and call me names. Finally, I called the police, he was arrested, and I filed for divorce.

The divorce was getting very ugly. He would use the court system as another avenue to negate the family order of protection against him and fight to see the kids—even though the kids were sometimes terrified of him. He then used the court system as a way to abuse the family. He used the kids as pawns to pull me back into the cycle of abuse. After going in front of the judge for the divorce hearing, we decided not to go through with the divorce because of financial reasons. After deciding not to divorce, I closed my hair salon and moved to Georgia.

Once again, we reconnected. Things seemed better for a while until his mood swings started again. Dr. Jekyll and Mr. Hyde was back. I rode the abusive cycle around and around and around with my abuser. Time periods between abusive explosions usually ranged from two weeks to around two days. The craziest episode was when he intensely emotionally and mentally tortured me. We were headed to New Jersey on a business trip. We got into a heated discussion about our business affairs, our marriage, and how I managed our household finances. He admitted that was not something he liked. During the conversation, I disagreed with something he said. As usual, if I did not respond the way he wanted, he became abusive and insulting. He cursed me out, called me all kind of names, and started road rage trying to run into an SUV, speeding at 100 miles per hour. I was terrified! I begged and plead with him to stop. He eventually stopped. I was so angry that I wanted revenge. When he stopped alongside the road to use the bathroom, I jumped in the driver side and locked the door. My intention was to leave him alongside the road, but he jumped on the step side of the SUV and held onto the top rack as I drove down the highway. The police station was up ahead, so I stopped there and we both went inside. The officer asks, "What happened?" I explained to him what happened and that we have a history of domestic violence. He checked the history and let me go. I then separated from him for some time.

When we decided to reconnect again, one day I asked him, "Why do you get so angry?" He said, "I witnessed my stepfather beating my mother." He said that his stepfather emotionally abused him and his mother. Through the years, I also learned my husband's biological father denied that he was his father. I attributed some of my husband's negative behavior to his dysfunctional family life but not the sexual perversion. Some of his patterns of behavior are attributed to his childhood. There were times in our marriage that he had no respect for me. He would call me some very explicit names in front of the children. I would ask him to leave. The next day, I would end up being the one who apologized.

In 2010, I was really going through a tough time. I was miserable and depressed. I had just found out my mother had died and to make things worse; my sister was diagnosed with breast cancer. He was not supportive at a time that I really needed him. I was empty inside with shopping as my addiction. These things happing in my life reminded me of how empty I was. Victor and I argued even more, and he became very distant. We separated once again. I then found out that we were going to be grandparents. This brought me so much joy at a time when I was going through so much pain. God does give us joy in the midst of pain!

After several months, we got back together again, but this time, he was worse than ever before. I found out he was having multiple affairs with younger women that I knew. When I confronted him, he started lying and manipulating. I asked him to leave. He became angry and verbally abusive. I told him it was over this time. I was done with the marriage. He was trying to grab me, but our youngest son got between us. I managed to call the police, and he was escorted out of the house with his clothes. He went back to New Jersey.

This was the final decision to end the cycle of abuse. We had been separated for over nine months; He admitted that he made mistakes, that he had changed, was sorry, and would make it up to us.

All he wanted was to get his family back together, and he would do whatever it took. He confessed to some of the affairs. He convinced me and those around him. I even gave him a 50th birthday party because I believed he had really changed and loved me. He started doing everything right, and I felt obligated to do my part to make our marriage work. But all of a sudden things got worse. Just like the other times, almost immediately, he was back to his cycle of abuse. The tension started building, and he began to mentally, emotional, and verbally abuse me to the point where I was emotionally drained. I found out he was still entertaining pornography; he was still conversing with the young ladies he had the affairs with. I decided it was over and told him to leave. He moved out. After him leaving, he believed as long as there was no actual physical violence, no domestic abuse had occurred.

It's extremely important to remember that no one knows the situation as well as the victim. It's been helpful for me to gain an understanding that my abusive husband chose to abuse me. In fact, it was during acts of abuse that he had the most power and control. Some people minimize the abuse that occurs, and this can bring about doubts in those of us who experience the abuse.

Abuse is a pattern of behavior used to control another person. The abuse can be physical, emotional, verbal, social, or sexual. Non-physical abuse does not always result in broken bones, black eyes, or cuts and bruises. Emotional and verbal abuse can break a person's spirit and his or her confidence and self-esteem. Abusers can be found in every economic group, race, and ethnic group. They include those who live in million-dollar homes and people who live in poverty.

People often ask about women who were battered: "Why doesn't she just leave?" This is a natural question, but perhaps it would be wiser and more insightful to ask, "Why does he abuse?" The complicated and dangerous process of getting out entails many challenges that people who have never been battered may not consider. When I wavered with the decision, I reminded myself of reality. For me, reality included broken promises and unbearable pain inflicted by my husband. To help me with my decision, I weighed the risks. If I divorced him, it is possible that I would remain single. If I stayed with this man, there is a very high probability that I would be abused again or dead.

Loneliness will be a painful challenge. However, I choose to be alone and safe rather than living in fear and abuse. In retrospect, my loneliest times were when I was married to an abusive man. I lost this man as my husband but gained safety, peace self-esteem, self-respect, health, the return of my personality, and my life. I live with physical and emotional scars that will never go away but wake up every day knowing that God has set me free from the yoke of bondage!

The abuser must take responsibility for his or her actions. Without accepting accountability for it and wanting to work to replace abusive behaviors with healthy ones, abusive partners can't and won't make lasting changes. I know because my husband still denies he has a problem and blames me. Even though I have suffered abuse, God is using my life story as a testimony. I hope anyone reading this can find the strength to leave. You are not alone. One should ever have to endure domestic violence. Are you called out of your situation and to speak up "FOR SUCH A TIME AS THIS?"

My mission now is to advocate for victims and survivors of domestic violence and sexual assault. I have started a movement for reclaiming our voice and compelling others to hear us. I will utilize information and materials to educate and give resources for women, men, and children to empower. I also wish to give them a comprehensive safe outlet, visibility, liberality how to break the silence and heal from violence in their lives! Join me! Speak Out!

I shared my domestic violence story with you to assist, encourage, and inspire you and to bring hope! If we don't tell our stories, no one will know what domestic violence is like as it hides behind closed doors! *"For God has not given us (survivors) the spirit of fear but of power, love, and a sound mind" (2 Tim 1: 7, emphasis mine).*

# Survival Talk...

## Journaling

Journaling helps us to release our thoughts and emotions. It can be a therapeutic tool that helps us along our journey. It offers clear structure in our goal setting and serves as an inspirational resource as we revisit to review our progression.

As I begin to journal my thoughts, I will see my progress.
From this day forward I proclaim that my life will never be the same.

I Survived!

# Chapter Five

## MOVING FORWARD, BLESSED AND FAVORED
### By Anitra Rose

As a child, I saw domestic violence all around me. But during those days, it wasn't called "domestic violence." It was called, "fussing and fighting" and that's just what married people did. At least in my family. I was told by my mom that her parents did it and I experienced my parents, some of my aunts & uncles, fuss and fight. Seeing that made me not want to get married at all.

During my teen years, I decided that marriage wasn't for me until one day someone explained to me how marriage could be a great thing when two people join together to be a team for God and bring Him glory supporting one another. That sounded good to me. And that's the kind of marriage I wanted. But it didn't exactly turn out that way. I met my husband through his father. We talked on the phone at first without him not knowing how I looked. But I saw a picture of him from his father. We talked about our past and the things we wanted in a future relationship. We seemed to have a lot in common. We finally met in person. Then one day out of the blue he shows up at my job dressed up in a suit to bring me a dozen roses. I thought to myself; "I could get used to this."

We continued to talk for a while but not seeing each other a lot because of his work schedule. I remember canceling a date and he was really upset, so we began arguing back and forth. That was a complete "turn-off" to me because it reminded me of what I heard and saw while growing up, and that's not something I wanted to deal with. I ended our relationship I expressed interested with someone else, but a year or so later became friends again. I was okay with just remaining friends at the time. But he eventually showed interest in me again. I wasn't sure about it but still decided to at least give it a shot. He told me his daughter missed and asked about me. I love her so dearly. He often said I loved "her" more than "him." And that I just wanted him to have kids with.

So I eventually saw his daughter more, met some of his family and parents. It seemed like we always had our issues about something. Always arguing and I always said, "Well, you ain't my husband!" I remember one time we were in the car talking and the discussion became heated, and we got into a big argument. I just remember my head being push into the window. I was shocked and pissed. I told him "No man was ever going to put their hand on me again so we can end this now!" I was so serious. I tried to get out the car, but he grabbed me saying he was sorry. That's the moment I should have ended it, but I didn't.

Shortly after that, he took me to the mall near where we lived, and as we were just walking around, we ended up going to the jewelry store. As we were looking around, we came across matching wedding band sets. He asked which one I liked. I picked two or three that caught my attention. Then he said, "Do you want to get it?" I looked at him and was a bit surprised at the question because I did not know. So, I said, "Ummmm, I don't know." In my head, I was thinking "Is this his way of trying to ask me to marry him? If so, he needs to do better." He continued looking and then finally asked me which one I liked the most if I had to choose. I made my final choice but was thinking in my head, "What the hell just happened?" I thought to myself that this proposal lacked the traditional stuff-- no bended knee, no romantic dinner, or no walk in the park. But, from that moment we just started making wedding plans. I was getting married, and I was scared as hell. My mom's response wasn't that great either. She was "old school" and questioned why he did not come to her first before asking to marry me. But when I called my dad; and told him the news, he said, "That's great!" he thought I may have had other news like being pregnant, but he was happy.

We started attending church together and took some classes on relationships for couples. It was there that many red flags showed up, and I knew that we had a lot of work to do before getting married. We were not ready, but we were going to get married anyway. Even with all the issues, red flags, and concerned family members, we still got married. We believed that whatever issues we have, they would work themselves out after the wedding.

I remember on my wedding day and walking down the aisle to "I Am Ready For Love" by India Ari. It was all like a daydream. I didn't know if someone was going to stand up when the preacher said: "If you think these two shouldn't be together let them speak now." That was my last chance, but since no one stood up, I took that as a sign that this was meant to be.

## Marriage Life

Getting married didn't change anything, except I couldn't use the line "You ain't my husband!" anymore. The same issues were there and did not disappear because we were married. They actually got worse. He thought that because we were married that he could control me more, and I started to think that since I was married, I would try to make the best of it. In the beginning almost every week I would put on nice lingerie, get him a card, and some wine and fix a nice dinner, but my efforts were unnoticed, so I stopped doing it.

He was a very aggressive communicator, who wanted immediate answers to all of his questions or he will keep talking and talking, and working my damn nervous. And If I tried to walk away, he would make me stay by blocking me from leaving or holding me. His aggressive way of talking to me was too much. There were times when I would go in the room and close the door. One time I jumped out the window and started walking down the street just to get away. I walked for a long time, and I didn't know where I was going. I just needed to get away from him. When he figured out that I left, he started blowing my cell phone up. I saw him looking for me, so I hid. When it began to get dark, I called my best friend, and she came to get me. We went back to her house, and I stayed the night, but I went back home the next day.

My husband was actually a "good man." He worked hard, loved his family and his daughter which I love to see, a man who loves his kids. But he would argue on the phone with his daughter's mom. I often wondered if they also had violent incidents. She was quick to say she would call the police if he started to act crazy with her; so I believe that she must have known something. He still tried to control her household even though they were not together.

I was a part of the dance ministry and the choir at my church which I loved. Well, eventually he told me God said for us to leave that church and we start attending his father's church. This was a major issue for me because I believe it was done on purpose, and I wasn't happy about his decision, but I went with it, trying to follow my husbands lead.

We had good moments and bad moments in our relationship. I got a new position working for the state government, but it caused me to work overnight, and although it brought in more money, it did not help our relationship.

I remember that the most fun we had in our relationship was during the time we were trying to conceive for the first time. We came home each day and made love. It was a magical time, and it worked! I was so excited when I found out I was pregnant and thought that everything would be alright. Wrong!!!!. After having our first baby together, things still didn't get better. I was still working overnight, and I had a little one to take care of. We argued about the smallest things and I was miserable. At one point I went to stay with my mom for a few months. But I eventually went back home.

We really tried to make things work out, but they just didn't seem to. Then, a couple of years later I ended up pregnant with my second child. When I told my husband, I had sparkling grape juice so we can make a toast and he just looked really "crazy" when I told him the news. I was very upset and just drank my juice by myself. He said he was shocked and then apologized but during this pregnancy, I didn't get a lot of support from him at all.

During this time, we continue the arguments. I remember one incident he wanted to talk about something while I was in the bathroom getting ready for work. I tried to walk past him out of the bathroom, but he blocked me in saying that we needed to talk. I continued to push past him, and he yelled at me saying "Why are you touching me?" He was holding me while I was trying to get out of the bathroom and I could have gone into early labor. Things became progressively worse after that because I discovered that I had to have brain surgery after delivering my son.

Six weeks after having a caesarean section I started having symptoms, and I went to the doctor. They told me that I might have a tumor on my brain, and I was bleeding in my brain, and I needed brain surgery. At this time, my child was only three months old, and the entire situation was so stressful. My recovery went well, except that I now had double vision. Apparently during the surgery, a nerve was hit that made me see double. I couldn't drive until it was corrected but I eventually regained my vision. I believe God needed more time with me. During that time, I sought him like never before. I believe that God will allow things to happen in your life to get your attention because He is a jealous God. I was so happy to be able to drive, but that privilege was taken from me again.

The following June, I had a seizure at my family reunion. That morning, my husband and I had another argument that began as something small but then escalated into a larger problem. I was a part of the committee for the family reunion and needed to pick up some items from the store. I asked if he could take the kids with him since there were only two people traveling in his car. He said, "No, take them with you." I was so angry, and I had not taken my medication at that point because I planned on taking them while at the picnic after I ate. But my body didn't understand that, and I had a seizure.

The incident that made me leave.

After I had the seizure, I could not drive for six months. I knew he probably was happy about it because I couldn't go anywhere unless someone else was able to take me, so I became very stressed. Eventually, I began an online relationship with another guy. He lived in another state, but I began to share all of my problems with him. The ironic thing is that one morning my husband decided to take me to breakfast because he said that he needed to talk. While we were talking, he announced that he had begun to talk to another woman online and was venting about his problems to her. He said that she wanted to get serious with him, so he cut her off. I honestly was not upset at this news because I just didn't "give a damn." I was like "Oh ok!" and he was looking like "That's it?" I thought to myself "Yep! Thanks for letting me know."

I continued to vent to my online friend, but eventually my spouse found out because one of his coworkers happened to be friends with the same guy and told my husband. When he found out, he called me at work and demanded to know the identity of my online friend, but I questioned him about why he wanted to know. He asked again and again, so I eventually told him. I knew it was going to be "hell" when he came to pick me up. So I had to prepare myself for the long conversation. While we were in the car, he began questioning me. We start arguing; I remember him saying he was going to crash the car. Knowing this, I said, "so you think killing both of us will solve the problem?" He explained that if he did that "at least we will be together." Hmmmm... WTH? That was a scary. He had actually turned the car as though he was going to drive off the highway and he had this look on his face as though he was possessed. But he actually did not veer away from the highway. We made it home safely but the arguing continued and began to escalate. While we were in the kitchen, he held me upside down with my face against the floor. I was in pain, and I told him that I couldn't breathe, but he would not stop so I began fighting back. When I was finally was able to get up, I grabbed a knife, and I told him to leave me alone. I kept it up so I can try to get out of the corner he had me trapped in. We wrestled some more as he try to hold me and make me talk. By this time, I had dropped my cell phone, and the battery fell out of it, and I could not find it. I was tired, so I told him I was going to bed. I got into the bed as he still was trying to talk and argue. He then climbed on top of me and forcefully had sex with me like that was going to make it better. I told him "No!" and he held me down. WTH!! I was being raped by my own husband! It was horrible and the worst feeling I ever experienced.

Eventually, I was finally able to go to sleep. The next morning which was literally a couple of hours later, he was ready to discuss the situation again. I was still very sleepy and really did not feel like discussing anything. While I was laying there, after I declined to talk, he put his hand on my lips squeezing them trying to make them move and said: "You are going to talk!" I attempted to push his hands away while yelling at him to stop simultaneously. I thought about my baby who was in the room, as we had a wrestling match.

Imagine wrestling with a man who weighed about 205 pounds and I only weighed approximately 125 pounds. He finally got me where he wanted me, and I couldn't get out of the position no matter how hard I tried, I was sore, my muscles were very tired I was so weak. He then took a pillow and starting smothering me. I was trying so hard to get up. I attempted to scream for my brother, but he

74

couldn't hear me. He kept pushing the pillow over my head; I was fighting for air. Then I asked him why was he doing this, what will killing me do. He said it would end the disrespect.

At this point, I had no more fight. I was about to die at the hands of this man. It was the scariest feeling of my life, the first time I had death knocking at my door slowly. At that precise moment, my baby began to cry. It was as if he was saying "Don't give up mommy, don't give up!" So I started to fight a little more. When he cried it snapped my spouse out of his possessed mode, and I was able to get up and grab my baby to calm him down. I was so shaken up and full of fear, and I knew I had to get away from him, but I still didn't know where my cell phone battery was after it fell out the night before. I wanted to call the police but couldn't because we did not have a "house" phone. I also did not want to tell my brother because I knew that he would confront my husband and that a fight would ensue. I had to immediately figure out a plan.

On the way to taking me to work, my spouse said something like "sometimes things happen." I simply responded by saying "ok" and was ready to go to work. At this point, I was full of a variety of emotions. Still shaken up, but I still had to try to get myself together and do my job. However, I told my mom and sister what happened, and they suggested a restraining order. I also called my best friend and told her what I experienced the previous night. She also felt that I should leave him and suggested that we come and stay in her home until things stabilized. She also said that she would take me to get a restraining order. I now had a plan.

The entire day I pretended that everything was okay (it was a Sunday) because I knew that on Monday morning I would be able to put my plan into action. I knew he would go to work Monday morning and after that, I could begin packing my belongings and everything the kids needed. I had to be gone before he returned home. I also hid the bag just in case he came home for anything (which he did). Once the "coast was clear," my friend came we loaded up her car with our things and were on our way.

When he returned home, he began calling my cell phone incessantly, but I wouldn't answer. I already knew that I could not go to my mother's house because that would be the first place he would look for me. And he did…he showed up and began to bang on the door until he realized that I wasn't there. He actually came to the house where I was staying, but they also told him that I was not there.

The next morning my friend watched the boys while I went to file for a Temporary Protection Order. I stayed with my friend for a few days but then thought it would be better if we stayed with my mom because she could help me with my children. So we relocated to my mom's three bedroom apartment. This only lasted a few months because it became very stressful for everyone living in such small space. My brother had also moved in, and there was limited space in the apartment. In addition, my family became a bit tired of caring for my kids while I worked and having to pick me up and drop me off at work (I was still unable to drive myself and work late). So in December, my six months ban from driving had expired, and I was able to drive, but I still had issues with childcare. There are not a lot of places that stay open until midnight but eventually I found a home daycare that could work with my time, but it was expensive for me. I couldn't pay this amount and try to find a place to live on my own. At this point, my spouse was not paying the amount of child support that he was ordered to pay by the court. I ended up changing shifts on my job, so I was able to get childcare and then apply to receive governmental child care assistance. It was then that my mom asked me to move back with my best friend because there were too many people in her house. I went back to stay with my best friend for a few months but, a conflict arose with her, and I had to leave. At this point, I really had no place else to go, so I returned home to my spouse temporarily. I told myself that it was only until I found an apartment. When I finally received approval for an apartment, I didn't have the money for the deposit and first month's rent so instead of staying there for a few days, I ended up living with my spouse again for a few months.

Moving back in with my spouse was very uncomfortable because I didn't know what would happen. I must admit that we did have sex a few times because I figured "he's still my husband, and I haven't had any sex for a while." However, it was the worst thing I could have done because being with him was just a bad experience.

When I moved back in things did not change too much from before I left. For example, there was a time when I won tickets to go to a concert, so I let my spouse know I had plans to go to the concert. When it was time for him to watch the children as I left, he told me that he would not watch them. He sat in the drivers seat of my car to prohibit me from leaving and from taking the kids. His father was there at the time as well, but he only made the situation worse. He (his father) began to call me "the devil" as I tried to take my keys from my husband so I could leave. It all went from "bad to worse" very quickly, so I ended up calling the police and my father. Although my dad was three hours away, I knew he would come if I need him to.

Once the police arrived, I told the police what was happening and after several questions, they determined he needed to be arrested. He was arrested in front of our kids which I felt horrible about, but it was something that had to be done. I also had to write a statement and give to the police. After the arrest, I started to move our things out of the house. I called my mom and sister to help, and I went to stay with them at my sister's boyfriend apartment. Again, I knew I had to come up with a plan as soon as possible. This was a temporary situation, and I needed a permanent solution.

After being there for a few weeks, I had to leave. I knew I had 2 choices --sleep in my car or go back to my spouse just for the night. I sat in the Walmart parking trying to figure out what I would do and decided to call a sister from my old church to inquire about shelters. We were not able to find any that night, so I returned to the house I once shared with my husband. I was so scared, but I went ahead and put the boys in their beds and slept on the sofa. I called and told him we were coming but didn't say how long we would be staying. Although I made it through the night, I did not have much sleep because I was worried. Thankfully he left in the morning before we did so I was able to take the boys to school and then contact the sister from church again to help me find a shelter.

After what seemed to be a thousand calls we were finally able to find a shelter with space for us. The woman there asked me questions and told me what time to arrive at the shelter with my boys. I called my sister In Christ and told her the news. I was nervous about the shelter because I had no idea what it would be like. I didn't know if it would be like the shelters I saw on television or if it would be different. What I did know was that if it did not work, we would be back at square one.

When we arrived, I was given a "tour" and discovered that the shelter rooms were like hotels rooms. We had our own room with three twin size beds and a bathroom, but the living room and kitchen were shared with the other residents. It was an interesting experience, but I believe all those women would rather be there than with their abuser. It was a friendly environment on most days, and I met some amazing women there. Some women came and left pretty quickly; I think that they didn't like curfew and sharing things or chores with others. It was a 30-dayshelter, and we stayed there about 33 days. My caseworker that was assigned to me knew about transitional housing program and thought I should apply for it. I was a little skeptical about the place because it was a good distance away in a town that I knew nothing about but I went ahead and applied for it. I was was accepted, we moved in, and we loved the apartment! It was perfect for us, and I knew that I was beginning the process of moving forward, and being blessed and highly favored.

Being a part of this program helped me tremendously. I received free counseling, and they had support groups every week. They tried to assistance in every way they can with the funds they have. My family and I are forever grateful. Many people think that leaving is the hardest part, but I also think that transitioning out on your own is the one of the hardest things ever. It something that I am still struggling with but I am grateful for the support I have received thus far. I still have a long way to go, but I probably would have gone back to my husband if I did not have these resources to help me.

Children may also be affected by a domestic violence situation. For example, my oldest son had a behavioral problem, while in school it seem as though they were trying to suggest he needed medication but I knew that wasn't the case. Instead, I worked with the faculty at his school, was able to get him counseling and with lots of prayers, he improved so much.

I honestly think that we still need more resources for domestic violence victims, and I pray I am able to support and help in that way. I hope and pray that others open up their hearts and help and support as well. That is the only way we will end domestic violence. I will forever bring awareness to this cause because through the grace of God I am a survivor. I want to help those who suffer in silence or fear. You can make it! I did and so can you.

Some church leaders tell you to "stay and work it out" but I believe God did not mean for us to be abused. Let's be clear about that. God allowed me to go through this to help others and because He knew I would give Him all the glory honor and praise. It's only by his grace that I turned this pain into purpose. If you know anyone who may be going through this, support them the best way you can. They need it. Help them find resources so they know it will be ok and if they leave and there is help available to them. Please don't belittle them or tell them it's their fault. They will leave when they are ready; you just pray that it's not too late.

Instead of walking in unforgiveness or being bitter by what I've experience. I choose to forgive, I choose to move forward, I choose to give God all the glory for bringing me through and I choose to share my testimony and use my pain for purpose.

# Survival Talk...

# Generational Curses

Though many of us may know of various events within our past ancestral history that can symbolize a generational curse, there are others that may not.

When we speak about *curses,* we may tend to think about some sort of 'witch-crafty' hex or a 'bad luck' black cloud—*if there is such a thing*. Generational curses are generally classified as ailments that are passed down to us from our generational past. History, which repeats itself over time through ancestry

What do the words 'generational curse' mean to you?

Do you know your family history?

Do your feel as though your life has been influenced by a generational curse?

What will you do to break the generational curses that plague your family?

# Chapter Six

## A SOLDIER'S TRIALS IN LOVE AND WAR
By Gabriel Fanelli

Psalm 4:8 In peace I will both lie down and sleep; for you alone, O Lord, make me dwell in safety.

I am a domestic violence survivor. More importantly, I am a father to three wonderful children who I love with all my heart. I have a unique story when it comes to domestic violence. I experienced all of my physical abuse as an active duty soldier in the U.S. Army. I have also experienced all of my recovery, success, and continual progress while in the Army. On October 12, 2015, I reached my five year anniversary in the military, and it marked the coming of another anniversary – two years free from abuse in my life. Therapy has taught me that you can never forget the things that happened. And we wouldn't want to. Our collective stories as survivors shape who we are today. But they don't *define* us. They are a part of us, but they are not all we are. If we allow our past to control our emotions, we allow our abuser to still have power over how we feel. This is about you. Your story as men and women who have been through "hell and back" and you are still here. Always look at your scars as proof that you were stronger than the thing that tried to kill you.

I grew up in Whittier, California and had a somewhat uneventful upbringing in a Christian home. However, I grew up seeing my mother and father yell at each other, and although it scared me and made me confused, it seemed like arguing was a normal part of relationships. Like everyone in this book, I never grew up thinking domestic violence would ever be a part of my future, other than seeing it in movies and television. On top of that, whenever I saw it in the media, it was always the image of a man hitting or screaming at a woman. I never had a concept that men could be abused at all. I think that's what most Christian men are brought up to believe. We never prepare men for what could happen if we are abused ourselves.

I was working as a manager at Sunglass Hut in downtown Santa Barbara when I met my spouse. She said she saw me a few times in town before she came into my store. Since I wasn't exactly focused on anything but school, work, and the church I wasn't accustomed to having a pretty girl come up and speak to me about anything other than buying sunglasses. We had our first real date at a wonderful little Italian restaurant in Montecito called Trattoria Mollie. I was still convinced I had to be romantic and pull out all the stops to get a good woman to love me. She kept saying she couldn't believe someone was treating her so well, she said her past boyfriends had been mean to her and not treated her well. I was convinced I was doing the right thing and treating her like a princess.

She was a more experienced woman, as I was still a virgin. Months of coercion led to a drunken night where she essentially raped me by going off into a tirade about how I didn't really love her. If I did love her, I would sleep with her, she screamed. She then forced herself on top of me, and I remember embarrassingly asking her "did you put it in?" and before I knew it she was riding me and I was giving up what I tried so hard to save until marriage.

Our relationship after that was defined by being physical. Nothing I did was ever right except sex. She began to do something that she would later do when we got married, use sex against me as a tool of manipulation. She would threaten to sleep with other men, flirt with them in front of me, and tell me that unless I did select sexual acts, she would leave me for someone else. Even my request to be allowed to use a condom was seen as a lack of love for her. Again, if I really loved her, she said, I wouldn't need to use a condom. Besides, she was on birth control.

These "if you really love me…" ultimatums are characteristic of high conflict relationship that involves domestic abuse or will grow into domestic abuse. There is never room for a middle ground, no place for discussion, and compromise is entirely frowned upon.

She became pregnant soon after, something she admittedly planned without my consent. A lot of credence is given to the "my body, my choice" mantra. For us men, that oftentimes ignores our choices and body. She was now pregnant and as bitter as I was, I quit school, joined the military and decided that I would give this child a good life with a father who is around. If you asked my spouse at the time, she would tell you otherwise – that I was a selfish man who didn't want the baby and didn't want to marry her. To a certain extent those feelings and emotions are valid in a situation like this, and I won't deny feeling both of those things at one point. But in the end, I suppressed them and did what I knew to be the right thing. For her, doing the right thing because it is right, and doing something for "love" were very different, and I would never be allowed to forget that.

I entered the service in October 2010, the same month I married her. I shipped off to basic training at Fort Benning, Georgia to become an infantryman. Our honeymoon phase consisted of handwritten letters while I was at basic training and this caused me to fall really in love with her. Maybe it was the old world romantic feeling that came with writing letters, or maybe I really loved her. Either was I was ecstatic to see her when she came out to see me graduate and go to Airborne school.

She stayed with me for three weeks while I was at jump school. My follow-on orders were to Fort Bragg, North Carolina. Since being married, I had only had these few weeks to really enjoy the marriage so far. It was a passionate three weeks full of promises of lifelong love and happiness. But we would soon move to Fort Bragg together, and I would enter "hell on earth." Nothing was good enough for her. Our three bedroom house was too small, she had no family close by, I was never home, etc. I was at a loss. We have both never lived in anything bigger than a one bedroom home, and when we met, I was living in a studio apartment. She also had the option to stay in Santa Barbara, as I was due to deploy to Iraq less than 30 days after arriving at my unit.

The night before I deployed, she told me she hoped that I would die in Iraq so that she could collect my $400,000 life insurance policy and "find a better man to be our daughter's father." Confused and distraught I didn't know how to react, but except to shut down emotionally and physically, I would arrive in Iraq feeling really ill. Also confusing was that a few weeks prior she had become pregnant with our second daughter. She had said another child was like her insurance policy in case I died she would have something to remember me by. Now she wanted me dead.

Our deployment was cut short from 12 months to seven after losing a friend to an improvised explosive device during a convoy outside Camp Taji north of Baghdad. He was the last American soldier KIA in Iraq. I came home and 11 days later, on December 31, 2011, my second child was born. She had Down Syndrome, and our lives would never be the same but in a good way. Having a child with special needs has been a blessing to me and taught me so much about communication, love, and compassion.

In the following months, her pre-deployment verbal abuses slowly turned into physical abuse. In addition, the verbal, emotional, and financial abuse was enough to drive someone insane. My debit cards were cut up, my ID was destroyed, and my uniforms were torn to shreds and urinated on. Our house was one huge mess of broken glass every night. The entire year of 2012 was a blurred timeline of various types of abuse. I averaged around three hours sleep a night when I was home, and when I went to train in the field I received the same amount, but my sleep quality was immensely better sleeping on the dirt in the North Carolina woods in the rain than next to my wife.

One way of control that abusers use is to cut us off from our families. Since my parents lived in two different states, I slowly lost contact with my family. She used to take my phone at the end of the day, and even sometimes at the beginning. I relied on friends at work to use their phones to call my mom and dad just to let them know I was alive. My parents knew I was being hit, but I never told them how badly. I was helpless in my own home.

My average day was enough to wear down even the toughest man. I would get up between 2:30 and 3:30 in the morning, depending if I got a ride or not. After morning (physical training (PT), I would get a ride home. My wife was usually still asleep. I would make the kids breakfast, feed them, and get them ready, then quickly shower and change for my actual work day. I would take the car if I could, but for her to be at home with our kids all day was unbearable for her. Since she had no concept of getting up early or respecting other's schedules, I would be late for work all the time as she told me she had to drive me to work since she would need the car. She never filled the car up with gas, and since our account was frequently negative, I sometimes borrowed money for gas from friends, or pushed it to the gas station and used what little we had.

There was only a handful of things which would anger her more than being rushed to get ready for the day. She would frequently say that she never joined the Army, so she would never answer to their schedule. As such, she made me answer to her. I was late ALL the time. My professional life, despite all my achievements, suffered greatly.

When she began to give me black eyes and would bruise my neck, arms, back and scratch my neck, I also began to get mocked at work. I was an expert infantryman, but I "allowed" my spouse to reign blows upon me without stopping her. To many, I was seen now as even more a failure than I already felt. Her taunting of me at home also increased. She knew that she had taken my virginity before I was ready, so she knew how important sex was – sex with her. She would bring up men she saw at the grocery store, on base, in town, and tell me that she wished she could be sexual with them. She would describe in great detail all the things she wanted to do with the men she saw. Many of the men she described were a part of the "Green Berets" where I could have been if she didn't force me to quit. The irony was lost on me; I was in shambles.

Her modus operandi was to taunt me, make me cower in fear by hitting me or coming after me and screaming. After she had me in tears by emasculating me and describing all those horrible things she would hit me some more as I begged for her to stop. At some point, she would stop, cry and tell me she was sorry. Then she would want to have sex. Sometimes she would want sex after she got herself worked up by talking about other men. It was as if this was some sort of sick game with her and I was her whipping boy. Sex was always her angle. No matter what she always ended her terror sessions with sex. A few times

I refused, and she threatened to go act out all the fantasies she said she had. I caved and had sex with her after being coerced. She confessed during an argument once to having sex with someone in our bed while I was deployed, but since she was pregnant, I would never know with who.

Her violence gained more confidence and more strength. She started hitting me in public. Once after failing to qualify for a new Toyota, she hit me so hard in from of a Toy's R Us store that I nearly blacked out. I got out of the Jeep and tried to run around the other side of the vehicle. She grabbed a box cutter from the glove compartment and chased me around. I begged her to stop. Bystanders going to shop with their children laughed as if this was just a joke. She began to choke me and dig her nails into me neck. She slammed my head into the window several times as our daughters were inside crying hysterically. Like a good little boy, I got back into the Jeep, and we went home. She later said she was so sorry for all she did. Again, sex.

Throughout our frequent violent episodes, I would still go to the field for a week to two weeks at a time. As much as she said she hated me and wanted me to die, she needed me. She frequently told me before I had a jump that she hoped the plane would go down or that I would break my legs or die on the jump. Anything to make me suffer. I was the only one to take care of the children, though. I made well over three-quarters of the meals for the kids. I bathed them every night, and I sang them to sleep. She was too busy with her "It Works Global" pyramid scheme business. Most of our money went there, and she never made a dime. In fact, she drove us into the negative seven out of the 12 months of 2012. Before I would go into the field, she would pack up all the bags for her and the girls and threaten to leave me if I went to work. Every time I left her was proof I was an absentee father in her eyes.

Army regulations only made my situation worse. Not only am I not allowed to defend myself, but the Army also has no way of defending me. If she was hitting me and I "bear hugged" her to get her to stop, that was considered a domestic assault on my part. If I blocked her from hitting me and she got a bruise on her arm by hitting me, that was also domestic abuse on my part. I had to "turn the other cheek" and try to escape the house. Many times I was backed into a room and blocked from any exit. I tried a twice to run out of the house and both times failed. One of the times she screamed after me, and when I turned around half a block away I saw her place my youngest daughter out on the cold pavement and screamed: "if you're a real man you won't leave your daughter!" I didn't, I couldn't. Another time she left the kids at home and followed me in the Jeep. She nearly ran me over until I came back home to find the kids by themselves.

In October of 2012, I brought my situation to the attention of my commander officer. The Army and the rest of the military to my knowledge have no means of protecting a male service member from domestic violence visited upon him by his spouse. There is a military protective order, similar to a restraining order but for the military. However, this order can only be worded so as to protect the spouse from the soldier. Since this is a binding legal document which, if violated, will find the soldier in violated of the UCMJ – Uniform Code of Military Justice – the document only has power over the soldier. No civilian, unless working as a Department of the Army civilian, can be prosecuted under UCMJ. When I came to my commander for help, they issued me a military protective order and did their best to word it to reflect my situation. I was removed from the home for the mandatory 72 hour period of no-contact the order covers.

October and December were the most violent months I would ever encounter. If I went to the field, when I came home at 1:30 am I would find the house a mess. She would come downstairs and slap me around telling me I never cleaned so it was up to me to clean the house or she wouldn't let me go to sleep. If she saw me sleeping on the couch, she would pour water on my face and hit me to wake me up. I felt imprisoned. I would sleep in a hallway closet with the door closed for safety. Sometimes I would sleep in the same closet because she would lock our bedroom door while I was putting the girls to bed. Usually, this meant sleeping in my uniform since I didn't get the luxury of changing and relaxing when I came home.

She began to tell me that she deserved to be paid for her services. She said she should be paid for cooking for the family, at the rate of a personal chef. She said she should be paid as a nanny, at the going rate. She also said she should be paid for sex at the going rate of prostitution. She was anything but a good mother or wife and when my kids would see her terrorizing me they would begin to cry and scream. I would always go over to them and put my arms around them. They needed to know it was still safe in the house, and I didn't think she would attack me so close to the kids. I was wrong.

On the afternoon of December 23, 2012, I truly thought I would die. She pushed me, and I stumbled halfway down the stairs before catching myself. She was going to kill me today; I was sure of it. I picked up my kids and took them into the laundry room with me and closed the door behind me. She opened the door, and I begged her to leave us alone. She grabbed my kids and put them back into the living room. They were screaming for her to stop now. I tried to get out of the laundry room, but she braced her hand against the door and began crying saying my attempt to get past her arm was hurting her. When I stopped, she swung at me and missed. She hit the door frame extremely hard and then blamed me. There was a fire in her eyes I had never seen before. She grabbed the broom as I passed her and went towards the front door. She swung the butt end of the wooden broomstick and hit me in the side of the head. I went down hard. I was dazed but not knocked out. I got back up, and she grabbed my hair and scratched my face and neck.

Over the next two years, I managed to get away from her and gain custody of my children, but only to lose it again when the current sitting judge in Monterey County took everything away from me in late 2014. I have since made the effort to come back from Colorado, where I had been stationed since November 2014, and fight for my children again.

The hardest thing for a victim before becoming a survivor is giving up the desire for justice. We want justice because once we're removed from the situation, we want the world to know what happened to us. Somehow if everybody else knows our abuser for who they really are, we will be vindicated. No, you will be enslaved, enslaved to the spirit of victimhood. Being a survivor is coming out the other side, fully remembering every gritty and painful detail of our ordeal, but not allowing the abuser to control us anymore by letting the abuse define us.

Trite and cliché phrases are born out of one of two things; ignorance or truth. A lot of literature written on the subject of abuse recovery and domestic violence does speak the truth, but its application is often ignorant. Only victims turned survivors know how difficult it can be to do what others see as simply "leaving." If there is one cliché phrase I can leave you with that I believe fully based in the truth is that you are not responsible for your abuse. Say it every day if you have to. Just as we wouldn't blame a defenseless animal for its abuser beating it, nor should we blame ourselves. I believe in fully taking responsibility for all of our actions, positive and negative. But taking the responsibility for our own abuse is a deadly trap which leads to years of mental anguish. You are not responsible for your abuse.

Remember, you are stronger than whatever tried to kill you. Embrace your scars, they tell a story. Courage, bravery, fortitude, and strength are not traits reserved for the knights of old, or the superheroes of the present. They aren't even traits reserved for those who have lived, fought and died on today's battlefields. These traits exist inside every one of us victims who have decided to turn into survivors. Our wounds tell a story. Our wounds do become wisdom.

# Survival Talk...

## Affirmations of Peace

Now more than ever, we want to maintain inner peace no matter what is going on around us. Therefore, we should not let fear control our lives.

Peace embraces me today

I deserve to be peaceful

With every breath, I become more peaceful

Peace surrounds me in everything that I do

The more love and peace I extend, the more I receive it

I deserve a peaceful life now

I feel peaceful and joyful

I create peace and harmony for myself

I accept peace into every facet of my existence

I choose to live a peaceful life today

I breathe in peace

I allow peace to penetrate every cell of my being

I live my life in peace

My dominant thought is peace

I resonate with power, peace, and love

Peace cascades through me like a waterfall

# Chapter Seven

**40 DAYS**
By Matrina Dorsey

If you had asked me five years ago if I was in an abusive relationship; the answer would have been no. But the Ugly truth is I was and had been for 18 years. You see I had been living an inauthentic life, one where I had to wear a mask in every social arena. The endless smile I wore would light up a room, but inside I was a broken spirit whose light had been drastically dimmed. I was verbally, physically, and sexually assaulted. All while having to raise two children in a financially controlled environment.

After much research and careful observation, I later realized that the obnoxiously loud arrogant man I had spent 18 years with possessed all the signs of a narcissist. In my darkest hour, I turned to God desperate for clarity, and it was placed on my heart to do a 40 day fast. I've entitled this chapter 40 days, because although domestic violence took 18 years of my life, it only took 40 days of complete surrender to step finally off of that emotional roller coaster. I've learned so much from my experience and marvel in the idea of touching, moving and inspiring others through my sharing. How can I share my experience leaving you touched moved and inspired in one chapter? It's difficult, but we will take this journey with the focus on how we met, the first incident and the moments leading up to my spiritual fast. As with any mental illness, most if not all of the symptoms are common, however, it is the severity of those symptoms that warrants a positive diagnosis. So as you journey with me, I ask that you put yourself in my shoes while paying attention to common similarities.

Was I smiling in my sleep? I ask my conscious as it slowly awakens. Sensing the movement of my lips as they take form in its upward position. I try to quiet the melody in my head...*It's the GOD in me,* by *Mary Mary*. Realizing that I'm a blink away from what most people view as consciousness, eyes wide open, I'm eager to get my morning started. I'm already dreading its end. Oh, how I enjoy the loveliness of nature before the sun completely rises. I feel closest to the omnificent one during this time, and besides that, it's the best time to shop Wal-Mart. That place is always busy. But first I must get out of bed!

Starring in the mirror, reminiscing the past, I think of my journey. Remembering when it all wasn't so clear. I recall asking myself, how did you get here and how could you have let someone treat you this way? I didn't understand then, but today I testify that God always has a plan. Thinking back on my experience, I can now see GOD's hand in what he does best, building character and preparing us for our future. It's all in his master plan.

It was the beginning of summer 1994, and I was working at Cracker Barrel, a country food restaurant chain throughout the south.

That was such a fun job. I made many lifelong friends there. I was only 20 years old, and I'm not trying to brag, but hey, I was a p.y.t., pretty young thing.

*I want to love you P.Y.T. pretty young thing*, is the melody in my head on repeat as I walk through the tight passageways of the gift shop. I'm dressed in the uniform: white button down shirt, khaki slacks and my brown apron labeled with four stars. Given the task of conducting all new hire orientations is a big deal, and I wear the four stars with pride. A 20-year-old college student with ten grand saved and not to mention a toned figure eight body. So yeah I'm a pretty young and smart thing. Michael wrote this song just for me, haha, or should I say "he he he" (in my Michael Jackson voice).

Sunday mornings are always busy, and I'm running back and forth from the kitchen to the gift shop filling to go orders and making sure everything runs smoothly. "Excuse me."

I hear a scratchy male voice from behind me. "What's your name?" I turn around with a fake smile on my face while hearing the words "jerk alert" going off in my head. My eyes bulge somewhat as I look at the character before me, and I do mean "character." It was live animation right before my eyes. He was wearing a mustard yellow suit, matching "fake" crocodile shoes and the biggest politician smile you could ever imagine. He was all the way live! "Hi, it's Matrina, may I help you with something?" He said, "I'm Joey, and I saw you over here looking so lovely. I just had to stop what I was doing and come over to speak." I responded in a sarcastic tone. I am so not in the mood for "Mr. Animated." Can't he see that I'm busy working here, I say to myself. Either he doesn't read body language well, or he's extremely slow because the next thing that comes out of his mouth is, "do you have a boyfriend"?

"No," I replied, "and I'm not interested in having one." I'd recently broken up with a high school sweetheart several months prior, and not quite over the hurt of losing love. " Take my number and call me, he said, I am new to the city, and I would love for you to show me around…just as friends." With a smirk on my face, I take the piece of paper, slip it into my apron, and walk away. That'll never happen; I say to myself.

Several days go by; I'm at work in my P.Y. T. zone as usual when I hear my name called over the sound system announcing a phone call. "Hello...thank you for calling Cracker Barrel."

I hear a scratchy imitation of "Jerome" a character Martin Lawrence plays on his sitcom *The Martin Lawrence Show.* "You can't call nobody," he says, "I've been waiting to hear back from you for days." I laugh and tell him that I can't take long personal calls at work. Up until now I hadn't given this guy a second thought. But I thought his "Jerome" impression was kind of cute.

This goes on for several weeks, the continuous calls at work and the funny character impersonations until he finally wears me down. I finally promise him a callback. I do, and we talk for hours.

*He is very charming and will give you a lot of attention early on in the relationship, making you feel as if the world revolves around you. The attentiveness will turn into possessiveness.*

Weeks go by, and conversation is continuous throughout the day. I wasn't used to so much attention. It felt nice! We met in July; it's now October and since our first date, Joey wants all my free time. This guy is like my shadow. The is different from anything else I've experienced. My high school crush was memorable, but I was always left wondering where he was or who he was with. With Joey, I didn't have to ask those questions; he was always with me. How can a girl not love all of this attention…right? Besides, Joey and I had a lot in common. We both were aspiring songwriters. You see I knew at an early age that I wanted to be a writer. I wrote my very first song, *Ocean Motion Lotion"* at the tender young age of five. This masterpiece was created one evening after my mother lotioned my body after a bath. From then on I'd answer, a singer, to every adult that asked what I wanted to do when I grew up. However, once I got into high school, I wasn't so quick to share my dream. I dealt with dysfunctional issues at home and somehow learned to suppress my feelings as I got older. Joey's boldness and ambition to make it in the music business were very attractive. It awakened that writer in me and although I was studying business, I was more determined than ever to make it as a songwriter. I felt as if God was guiding me to my destiny.

Joey pops the question! It's only been three months, but we are always together, and our union seems to have a purpose. He's so charming, and everyone seems to like him, so I accept his proposal, and we are now engaged. Several months pass and I miss my period. A trip to the doctor confirms a pregnancy. Joey seemed so happy, and his excitement put me at ease. Afraid to share the news with my family, I held off a while. We weren't married yet, and my dad wasn't sold on Joey. "He seems to lust and not love you; there's a big difference," he said. Against his better judgment, he allowed us to move in to help out. Joey didn't have a stable income and with a baby on the way we needed to save money. With his charming personality, he promised to do right by the baby and me. This put my dad at ease.

During the pregnancy, Joey was so attentive. He rubbed my feet and catered to me in every kind of way a girl could ask. But it wasn't until after my son was born that I realized something wasn't right. What first appeared as attentiveness was now bordering possessiveness. He blamed the constant check-ins on wanting to make sure the baby and I were ok. "We are just fine," I would constantly reassure him, but the calls were continuous when we weren't in sight. If I didn't answer, he called family members, checking to see if I was there. He didn't stop until he tracked me down everywhere I went. Joey also began to start arguments over silly things. What was for dinner, or why the kids weren't asleep. It was as if the smallest things ticked him off. Up until the pregnancy, I was able to calm him down with a simple smile or a back rub; but Joey is now very short tempered, loud and obnoxious. The man that I once knew as charming and attentive had now become detached and very controlling. It wasn't long before the first physical incidence.

We are still living with my dad when the Braves won the World Series in 1995. The city is on fire, and diehard fans are tomahawking through the streets of Hotlanta. Joey decides to go out with friends and celebrate in my brand new creamsicle orange Mitsubishi Eclipse. We need a reliable car for the baby he says, as he looks for me to finance the car payments. Everything we've financed so far is in my name since he filed bankruptcy just before we met.

While Joey's out celebrating, I'm home doing laundry. A tiny crumbled piece of paper hits the floor. My heart drops. It's a girl's phone number. Trey isn't even a year old, and this man is out in the streets collecting phone numbers. I'm pissed, but more than that, I'm so very disappointed. I knew we had our issues, but cheating was a deal breaker for me, well, at least, that's what I told myself. Later that evening Joey made advances for sex. I was not about to have sex with a man that suspect for cheating. Joey was very upset with my refusal. But I gave him the silent treatment.


*Studies suggest that narcissistic men become physically abusive when denied sexual gratification.*

My girlfriend had invited us to a baby shower the next day, so I prepared for the outing. The phone number I'd previously found was heavy on my mind. I didn't want to jump to conclusions, but I needed answers.

The car's all loaded and we're heading to the shower. Joey's driving and I'm blessed with the sweetest gummiest grin as I turn and check on my bundle of joy in the backseat. I'm so determined to give him the best, and I know that kids typically have better foundations in a two parent household. I want that for my son. But the phone number I found in Joey's pocket is eating me up inside. His infidelity could ruin everything. I can't do this silent treatment thing anymore. I have to know, I ask Joey... "I was doing the laundry yesterday and found Sheree's phone number in your pocket, care to explain"?

His body language screamed busted. Very irritated by the question, he answered in a very condescending tone as if I didn't have the right to question him..." and, so what," he responded. "So what! I replied, why do you have her num"... And before I finish the statement, I feel his hand go across my face...whack! I'm in disbelief! My head hits the passenger window. The sting of the slap has my face burning, but the rest of my body feels numb. Everything is moving so slowly, and I feel as if I'm in a dream.

As I come out of the fog I can't stop myself; my first reaction is to charge him. Reaching out   with the intent of giving him something he can feel, he blocks my blow, throwing out his fist and punching me in the arm.   This cant' be happening, I say to myself. My mind is racing, and I can't keep track of my thoughts.  Joey seems possessed.  He's shouting, and his eyes are bloodshot red.  His veins bulge out of his forehead and neck.  With the car swerving, he says in a desperate tone "I'll kill us"…. he had lost it.

Kill us?  not my child!  These words brought me back to reality.  I turn to look at baby Trey crying in the backseat.  I realize that I have to gain control of the situation.  Holding back the tears, in a desperate but yet commanding tone, I plead with him to calm down and stop the car.  I remind him that our son is in the backseat.  I guess that brought him back from his trip to hell because he finally started to calm down.   I finally bring myself to a place where I can reach back and comfort the baby.

He's finally calm, and I'm feeling the tiniest amount of relief. It feels as if we've been driving forever.  I don't want to get him started again, so I don't utter another word.   Starring at the cars passing by I try to make sense of what just happened.  With my lips parted slightly and gently shaking my head left to right, I slowly inhale, feeling my chest rise…and from the depth of my soul I exhale. The baby's finally quiet, and my mind starts to roam.  Who is this man, I ask myself?  I've been sleeping with the enemy.  I can't stay with him.  What am I going to do?

I notice that we've turned into my girlfriend's neighborhood. How am I going to face her, I ask myself?  Tiffany is a friend I met working at Cracker Barrel. She was actually there the day I met Joey. He had her, and everyone else fooled with his award winning charming act.

He turns down her street and parks the car in front of her neighbors' house. And in a condescending tone, he turns and say's, "I'm sorry that happened," all while shrugging his shoulders. "I'm under a lot of pressure trying to get us out of your dad's house. I meet a lot of people in the business, and it's all about who you know...we're trying to build something Trina...I'm doing this for us..."

This is his excuse?... I say to myself. He meets a lot of people in the music business?... and for that reason I shouldn't question phone numbers? What about the fact that you were just a deranged, violent man moments ago? I'm dealing with a real-life *Dr. Jekyll and Mr. Hyd.* I'm beside myself. My head is spinning.

At that moment, I noticed my girlfriend walking towards us. She saw us sitting in the car and assumed we needed help with the baby. "Hey guys," "need any help," she said with an eagerness to do so. Joey jumped out of the car, embraced her with a smile, made some type of funny remark and laughed hysterically. His demeanor was completely different, and he seemed totally unaffected by his previous hellish behavior. I didn't want my girlfriend to know what I had just experienced. I didn't want to spoil everyone else's day. Yes, I'm that girl who's there for my girlfriends when they need me. I am also that girl who faces many issues alone. So following Joey's lead, I pull myself together. I smiled, I laughed, and I engaged in conversation. Looking back today I realize that this was my introduction to "the mask." I didn't know it then, but the "mask" was soon to become a permanent fictional character in my life.

Joey was continually apologetic months after that episode. He seemed somewhat genuine at times but in a sarcastic overly confident way. It was as if he embellished in the idea that he was   deserving of my forgiveness. Asking for it at times, and then taking it back if I didn't respond the way he anticipated. But I didn't want to lose my family, and besides, it's not as if I hadn't seen a man hit a woman before. I was all too familiar with keeping family quarrels  behind closed doors. Childhood memories of my parent's scuffles were buried in my subconscious. After giving Joey the silent treatment for days, I broke down and forgave him. I realize today that this was the beginning of the violence cycle.

Shortly after this incident, I learned I was pregnant with my daughter. My family wasn't happy about this. They felt as if Joey was using me. You see Joey, and I were pursuing careers in the music industry. I had  dropped out of school in pursuit of this career path. I worked a corporate job while Joey continued to network in the industry. Both my dad and brother voiced their concerns. So I wanted to prove that I was capable of making good decisions. I was determined to make it work, not just for our family but for our dreams.

Joey found a place out in the suburbs. I didn't want to move so far away from my family, but the school system was better there, and so I didn't put up much of an argument. His credit was still shot; so I ended up financing furniture for our new place. Before long I had accumulated over 20 thousand dollars of debt. Joey was so convincing when he told me not to worry about it. "That'll be nothing to pay off once we get going in the business," he said. He swore that the kids and I were his world and that he would always take care of us. I trusted him. Looking back, I realize that moving so far away from family wasn't a good idea. It's very common for abusers to isolate their victims from friends and family.

Years go by, Joey, and I still haven't had our big break, and although I've become numb to the abuse, God's grace keeps me. I should've been an actress because I was so good at pretending everything was great. Time spent with friends and family was time away from him, and he kept me on a short lease. I spent most of my time at home to keep down commotion, and it wasn't long before I found myself completely alienated. His words were like weapons. I was constantly belittled. His arrogant behavior was loud and obnoxious and created an environment of tension and disease. Every argument didn't become physical, but he knew how far to go to make sure I knew what he was capable of. I wasn't in control of anything, not even my own body. I often turned to God in times of despair; I prayed for peace. My prayers were always answered. God has a way of bringing tranquility in the midst of a storm, and this made me feel special, it made me feel loved.   Although my house was not a home and hell was all around me; God's love was planted in my heart, and I rested peacefully in knowing this to be true.   Even after a sexual assault.

There's nothing worse than being sexually assaulted.  Trust me, it's the worst feeling in the world.  Especially when it's done by the one person who should be protecting you.  I can still remember the moments leading up to the first time I was violated.  An old girlfriend invited me to her wedding events.  As soon as the invitations arrived, Joey started investigating.  Co-workers would question my reason for calling just to hang up during late night hours. I knew it was him, screening my calls while I slept.  He had even broken into my voice mail system at work.  I was under constant surveillance.

Leaving the house without the kids or Joey was difficult, he made every attempt a dramatic event.  On the day of the bridal shower, Joey started a huge fight accusing me of cheating on him.  I can imagine how treating someone this poorly can bring about unwarranted insecurities. "You ain't  shit," he said. "You're just a groupie, your ass ain't going to a bridal shower,  you're trying  to lay up with somebody."  But I told my girlfriend I would be there, and my intent was to honor my word.   It's funny how promises made to others take priority over the ones we make to ourselves. Think about it!  In an attempt to rattle me, Joey took my keys and parked the car the next street over.  I was so disgusted with life. This was too much!

I had cut myself off from the outside world long enough and was determined not to miss my girlfriends bridal shower. After much arguing, I grab my things, kick off my heels and walk a street over to my car before finally leaving for the event.

I can barely catch my breath and not to mention completely emotionally distressed. Why do I have to go through so much drama just to leave the house? I feel like I've gone through WWII! Emotions take over, and I can't hold back the tears any longer. Driving seems impossible. Pulling into a park near the Chattahoochee seems like the best place to get my composure. Water has always been my ultimate calming agent. Sitting there, I pull down the car's sun visor and stare at the woman I see in the mirror. I promise her that I will take my children and leave.

I never made it to the shower. I just couldn't seem to pull it together. Feeling overwhelmed with distress, I decided to go back home. I just wanted to be near my babies. Joey hurried downstairs when he realized I was home. Frantically pacing the floor, he started arguing again, this time accusing me of sleeping with someone. "I will see for myself," he said. Hurrying up the stairs, I close and try to lock the bedroom door. Blocking my efforts he pushes his way into the bedroom and throws me on the bed. I can tell by the look in his eye that he's about to force himself on me. Crying uncontrollably, I beg him to stop! He tears off my underwear and forces himself inside me. He then looks down at me and says that he could I'd been with someone else because my pussy was stretched out. I'm sickened, disgusted and feel so unbelievably violated. I go to my quiet place with God, reaffirming my intent to leave. Asking myself how was I going to make this happen. Not only am I emotionally distressed from being in a cycle of both mental, and physical abuse but I'm also financially trapped.

Trapped in the violence cycle, Joey goes through the apologetic stage again. But that didn't stop him from threatening never paying off the debt we had accumulated in my name, over twenty thousand dollars, remember; or ever offering financial help with the kids. But I had made up my mind, I was leaving!

Months go by, and I've saved enough money to leave. I knew that I couldn't give him any indication of my plan. Leaving the house for work was difficult enough, so I could imagine how difficult leaving for good would be. I decided to create a monthly budget and sat down one evening to go over my finances. My heart dropped! Joey had somehow gotten into my savings and spent most of the money. Inspector gadget had figured out my intentions. I couldn't believe it. Appalled at the audacity of this man to steal from me, I confronted him. This, of course, led to a major argument, but this time, I had built enough courage to ask for help.

Angry at the idea of me questioning him about my money, Joey grabs a knife out of the kitchen and backs me into a wall. With the knife at my throat, I can't stop thinking of my kids upstairs. Praying that they didn't come down to witness this horrific scene, I got my wish. They were sound asleep. I somehow get away and lock myself in a bedroom. Moments pass, and I hear him unlocking the door with the key I had hidden. He walks in calmly and starts apologizing. As he reaches out to hug me, making sexual advances; I push him away. This man is crazy; I say to myself. There's no way I will allow him to force himself on me again. He then tries to kiss me and rub his hands between my thighs. I wanted to throw up. I refuse, and he tries to pin me down. I shuffle my way out of the room, grabbing my phone, and dial 911. His jaw drops. I had never done that before.

The police came and talked to both of us. I explained why I called, and they said that it was a domestic dispute and that they wouldn't get involved. I was actually ok with that response. I didn't want to send him to jail. I just wanted him to respect my wishes and allow me to leave peacefully. That wasn't the last time he tried to force himself on me, but from then on I would threaten to call the "po po" and that would stop him in his tracks.

Breaking the silence is the first step to recovery. Months go by, my savings are gone, and I'm desperate to leave. I had worn my mask for so long, but somehow I was able to bring myself to an authentic moment. Reaching out to the family was difficult, but they were very understanding and supportive. I rented a Uhaul truck, pulled up to the townhome we were leasing and told Joey I was leaving. Ironically that morning I denied him sexual gratification. This started Joey on a rant, saying his mistress was moving in, and he wanted me gone. So when I returned with a U-Haul, he seemed somewhat shocked but calm. He even gestured to help my brother, and I pack. I asked my mother to be there as a peacemaker, and my niece was recruited to take the kids away. However, it wasn't long before the drama started. Joey begins acting foolish over the furniture. Now, remember, I had accumulated thousands of dollars in debt for this furniture, but he was taking claim to everything. He threw his body over the dining room table, refusing to move. He grabbed all the pictures off the walls, running through the neighborhood frantically stashing them someplace where we couldn't find them. I was completely outdone and over his madness. I took what I needed, and we left.

On average, a woman will leave an abusive relationship seven times before she leaves for good. This was the first time I left Joey, but it wasn't the last. I felt a major sense of loss. I know it seems strange to feel this way, but my life with Joey was all I had known as an adult. This dysfunction was my normal, and it's very difficult to walk on the other side of normal. Joey got counseling from a minister friend that he had been working with and convinced me to come back. I know now that God was still preparing me. I hadn't quite learned his lesson. I begged him not to give up on me.

It's the year 2012, and I can't believe I've given this man another 12 years of my life. I've been on this roller coaster for so long that I can't see my way out. God has always been here, keeping me sane, but I'm in my darkest place, and I need clarity. I need to hear a voice, a whisper, a sound. I was desperate for his guidance. It was placed on my heart to do a 40 day fast; an act that had been done for centuries by individual's seeking wisdom and protection from the highest GOD. All I wanted was a mere spiritual intervention. I asked God to intervene and to heal my family if it was his will. If not, I asked for signs, I needed clarity on his desire for me to move. I asked for the strength and the courage to obey his will.

My friends, during my 40 days fast God revealed everything I needed to know. Looking back, I now realize the miracle that I received. I had been trapped in a continuous abusive cycle, experiencing all form of abuse: mental, verbal, sexual, physical and financial. I question myself often, wondering how a 40 day spiritual fast delivered me from an 18-year mind trap. On that 42nd day, I packed my things, and I left with the sure notion that I was in God's will.

God placed a calling on my heart. After my deliverance, I looked to the heavens, resting in the comfort of knowing that I remain in his presence and forever connected; I asked God what he wanted from me. I knew he didn't reveal himself to me this way, answering my request for signs, for my satisfaction only. God wanted something from me. If we seek him with sincerity, he will reveal himself. He craves a relationship with us. It was placed on my heart to share my story. I was to advocate for this cause. I was to bring awareness to the ugly truths surrounding domestic violence and what to expect from a narcissist ex.

It's been three years, and I'm still a work in progress. I heard a philosopher say that character growth extends from the struggle. Well, I should be full grown by now. Leaving is only the first step and leaving a narcissist like the character is comparable to starting a war. Now that I'm aware of the textbook characteristics, my goal is to help both men and women recognize and prepare for that journey; transforming them from reactive victims to proactive survivors. I mentioned earlier that if you had asked me years ago if I was in an abusive relationship, my answer would have been no. Today I live in my truth. My prayer for you is to live in yours. Breaking my silence was the first step to recovery, and so I leave you with a quote that I believe will save millions: Break the silence, and break the cycle. Become a truth speaker.

# Survival Talk...

# Overcoming Fear

*Looking back over our lives to clearly see how we have allowed our fears to shape who we are and the world around us.*

Fear is not bias to age, social class, financial status, race, creed, color, nor sexual orientation. It doesn't matter who you are or what you do; you are not exempt from fear. Oftentimes, our fears are created as a result of our childhood experiences; which carries on with us throughout our adulthood. Especially in areas that deal with matters of gravity, world destruction, situations of physical harm/abuse, or imposed fear from others. These haunting reservations become the canvas for the portrait of lives.

**Recognizing the different types of fear**

- *Emotional Fear*
- *Spiritual Fear*
- *Mental Fear*

- *Physical Fear*

- *Social Fear*

- *Worldly Fear*

Fear can bring about a number of "disabling" emotions such as shyness, doubt, isolation and lower our self-esteem. This is why we may tend to feel unfulfilled. The Bible tells us that fear was not a part of the 'blueprint' that God used when he created us. Considering this, we have to be careful about letting fear hinder our lives.

Why do you fear?

What do you fear most?

At what age did you realize your fear?

How do you respond to your fear?

Who or what inspired you to overcome your fear?

My life will no longer be ruled by fear…I survived!

# Chapter Eight

## A REBELLIOUS LOVE
By Brenda Gonzalez

" You will allow, what you are not aware of. Love will blind us, from the pain inside of us."

I was fourteen years old the first time I saw him. I was walking to my first-period class P.E., which was tennis. I guess I've always been a sporty girl. I have always liked to challenge myself in learning new things.  So, I challenged myself in learning a new sport. Plus, I didn't think  many teens would be interested in learning tennis. I thought it would be an easy class.  Never realized how much coordination was needed and how interesting it would be.

He said: "Hi" to me, as he tried walking next to me until I got the tennis court. I was totally ignoring him. I thought to myself, this guy really has some nerve to be trying to talk to me. I was not attracted to him one bit.  He was short and not my type.  I walked faster to get to the tennis court so that he could disappear out of life.

To my surprise this would not be the last time, I would see him. He was also on my brother's soccer team.  He had become friends with my brother and his crew and now started hanging out, around the area we all did during lunch. He always tried talking to me. I would ignore him all the time. As time passed by he kept being persistent. It was annoying but fun at the same time. After all, some girls like to be the center of attention especially when broken from the inside. I found out that his best friend also liked me. It was as if they both were in a competition to try to get with me. Who doesn't love those high school days, it was all fun and dandy.

What caught my attention from him was his grouchiness and that he was very persistent. He was always angry and bitter about life. I thought maybe I could fix him and be someone good in his life. I became vulnerable to the attention that is given to me. I was in the need of love and attention. I could not see that I was also angry and bitter about life. This is why I attracted him.

I finally became his girlfriend, after only two weeks he broke up with me. I didn't want to kiss him, and he got so upset he broke up with me. Eventually, we got back together. This would be the first break up of so many that would come throughout the years I was in this relationship. Signs always show up right away, and we blindly miss them. I also discovered that my mom didn't like him because he was short and not good-looking.

I was your typical rebellious fourteen-year-old and loved doing the total opposite of what my mom wanted me to do. So to piss her off, I became his girlfriend again and started spending time with him during school.

As time passed, I began to like and eventually learned to love him. Sex became an addition to us. Every chance we would get we would have sex. I guess at that age I confused love with lust. It was something I was doing for the first time, and it felt good. When the relationship began to get too serious, my mom stopped allowing me to go out to the house parties to avoid us from being together. This eventually backfired because I began to ditch school to hang out with him. At the age of sixteen I came up with the brilliant idea to get pregnant, so she would not be able to separate us. As I planned it out, I got pregnant at the age of 16. So many of my friends told me to get an abortion. I totally refused the idea. I honestly had no clue what I was getting myself into. But knew that I couldn't abort my child.

When I was about three months pregnant, he talked to my mom and told her I was pregnant, and that we decided to move in together. I never had the nerve to talk to my mom. I left without facing her. I just grabbed my things and left my house. I knew I was wrong and didn't have the courage to face her. We left to live to his aunt's house in Fontana, which is a city far away from where I currently lived and went to school. The aunt was very nice and supportive. It was weird to be there all alone. I would drive to school every day. It would take me about two hours every day. This was so hard for me. It scared me because of the possibility that I could get into a car accident because I would become very sleepy while driving.

He had dropped out of school in the middle of tenth grade. He tried getting a job nearby where we lived. Unfortunately, there weren't too many job opportunities out there. It was a small city, and it did not offer too many options. He kept working for a carpet cleaning company in Los Angeles. He had been working for this company for a few years with his step-father. This job allowed him to be out of the house all day, and I barely saw him.

After three months of living with his aunt, we moved out to our own apartment in Hollywood. It was a single bedroom, but it was pretty big, and it was only the two of us. This made me feel happy. I was finally going to see him more and be closer to my school and family. I was happy that he was working, and I was able to continue with my education. But nothing really changed. I would hardly see him. He would work his regular job and also cleaned carpets on his off time for extra money. I guess I should had been thankful, but as a teen, I didn't understand any of this. All I wanted was to spend time with him. The man I thought I loved and was about to have a child with.

I remember one day he told me he had to do a side job. He left really early that day and was gone most of the day. When he returned home, he went to clean a neighbor's carpet. He left his pager on the table, and it started to buzz non-stop. I got curious and called my sister-in-law to call this number. Just as I suspected, it was a girl. He had been with her all day long. She even described what he was wearing that day. She also told my sister-in-law that they been seeing each other for a few months. I was so furious and so upset that I began crying uncontrollably. I felt like my whole world was ending. I was six months pregnant at this point. Never in the world would I have imagined that this would be happening to me and that it would

122

be the first of many affairs that he had, that I would find out about and still forgive him.

When he returned home that night, I confronted him and asked who this girl was. I wanted to know how she knew what he was wearing that day. I was crying and yelling at the top of my lungs. He tried to tell me to calm down. He kept telling me to remember that I was pregnant. I thought "Did you remember I was pregnant when you were out with this girl all day?" As many men would, he denied the whole thing. I slapped him and ran out the door crying. I can't even imagine how crazy I must have looked. I can't remember how many blocks I ran through the streets of Hollywood, and no one ever stopped to ask if I was okay or to see if I needed help. I finally returned home, and he apologized to me. He said it meant nothing. I was sixteen years of age and six months pregnant, so I wanted to believe him. I wanted a family, and I loved him so much. Or at least, it is what I believed was "love" at that time in my life. I wanted to change the repeated cycle of our families. My parents divorced when I was about six, and he never met his dad. I wanted a family and believed I could do this. I was determined to do the impossible to have a family.

Several months passed by and I gave birth to my daughter. It was the most magical thing. I felt like I finally had someone to live for and try to accomplish things for. We soon moved to a different apartment to be closer to my school. At this point, I was in the 11$^{th}$ grade. I was going to a continuation school that allowed me to take my daughter. It was good to be around people my age but also be able to spend time with my little princess.

Nothing really changed at our home, though; he still would go out. He would come home late from work, and I would always confront him. Most of the time he was drunk so things would always escalate after a few exchange of words. It never failed I would cry, yell and end up slapping him because I was so angry. He would always beat the crap out of me then feel bad and apologized. It became such a routine. One day it was so bad that he thought he had broken my nose. He did not allow me to go to school. He iced my nose all day and kept asking me for forgiveness.

I honestly believed he was sorry and forgave him each time. I never told anyone out of shame or maybe because they would tell me to leave and at that time I did not want to. I wanted to believe that this would get better, that we could still have the happy family I've always wanted. Your mind starts adapting to the possibility that this is "love," and its okay.

As the years passed by, things got worse. My daughter was older, and she began to witness all the fights. She would panic and start yelling the minute she would hear us fighting. She always knew what came next. I still could remember her little face full of fear and would yell to try and get our attention. How selfish were we as parents sometimes to put them through these situations because we think it's normal. We think this is the way love feels. We are so broken inside we can't recognize how much we are bleeding internally.

I had gained a lot of weight over the years, and I would do some of the craziest things anyone can imagine. I would threaten him that I would throw myself out of the car as he was driving. I would show up to his friends house looking for him. You named it; I did it. I was scared and lost. I would go to nightclubs and try to catch him with other women.

I often would ask myself "why don't you leave him?" But then I would also ask myself these questions "Where would I go? What would I do? How would I raise my child?" I was still in school. Those questions occupied my head all day long. The fear of hearing "I told you so," from my mom. At this time, it felt good to be in school and surrounded by people my age. I never told any of my friends or teachers of what was going on at home. Maybe I felt guilty that I always started the fights and that I would be the first one to lay hands on him, and it was my fault that I was beaten. I was hurting so much every day. The thoughts were very heavy on my heart and mind. I couldn't focus anymore.

I finally had the courage to leave. We had broken up numerous times but had never actually separated. I felt it was best for both and our daughter. We couldn't continue this lifestyle. Although my heart was broken, and I felt like a failure, I refused to show emotions around my daughter. I wanted to portray I was a strong woman but only I knew I was dying inside and would cry every night. Once my daughter was in bed, I would sit outside the apartment and smoke cigarettes. I felt though I had failed as a woman, mother, and partner. We often blame ourselves when things fall apart. I would tell myself "If I had only not said this or that." Or, "If I had not slapped him." It's crazy how much we can torment ourselves with the negative thoughts in our head. I really believe that I had failed at keeping my family together.

While in the sixth month of separation, I decided to go out with my friends. We went to out to a nightclub in Hollywood and to my surprise, I ran into my ex there. It was awkward at first. We talked to each other and danced. Then, a girl came over to where we were sitting and kissed him in front of me. Inside, I was very upset, but I knew we were not a couple so I really couldn't say anything. We continued partying throughout the night and next thing you know we were having sex at his apartment.

We didn't talk about that night again until I found out I was pregnant again. We decided to get back together and try this again for our children. Things seemed to get better for a few months. He still had the same job, so he was still continuing to go out and come home drunk. It was like a cycle that would never end. I was so young and immature. He would beat me up and threaten to leave me. I would be crying and begging this man not to leave me. I would force myself to have sex with him so he wouldn't leave me. I had no self-respect and felt as though I did not have control of my actions. I was bitter and angry all the time. I think that we do crazy, dumb things for the men we think we love. We keep trying to fix our brokenness with sex. I think I was going crazy. He was not only physically abusing me, but he would also verbally abuse me too. After my second child, I had gained a lot of weight, and I was over two hundred pounds. He would say things to me like: "You are a mission impossible." And, "You will never lose weight." My self- esteem had always been low so it was so easy to believe all the lies he would tell me. He would say, "No one will ever love you the way you are or the way you look."

Our neighbors would call the police on us when the arguments would become too loud. I'm surprised they never took him to jail, nor my children away from us. I often wonder how many cases might have gone under the radar because cops would not really care enough or address the situations better. I began to question if the police were properly trained to deal with domestic violence? Didn't they think it was dangerous because we were so young?

After having my son, we moved into the back house of my mom's house. We decided that this would save us some money so we could buy our own house. We now had two kids, and we were trying to make this family work out. I truly believed he would not have the nerve to hit me there. However, nothing really changed there either; my mom could hear us fight from her house. I was super loud, and I honestly didn't care. I mean who has time to worry about neighbors when you are upset and fighting. I know I didn't. When things would elevate, it was always my fault for being mad and yelling. He never took the blame for the things he was doing to destroy our family. I think that men tend to do that to you; they make you believe it's all your fault. You're the "loud" one, the one with the "attitude," the "bitter" one, and it was always me and never him. It was a repeated cycle year after year.

The days that he would try his hardest not to hit me he would punch holes in the walls or the kick the doors. I don't think my son witnessed as many fights as my daughter did. She always had the same panic attack when she would hear us argue. Things kept getting bad between us and we hardly did any family things together anymore. He was always either be working or watching television, but that never stopped me from taking my kids to places. Even at a young mom, I kept them involved in sports and activities. I tried my best to be the best mother I could be, but it was really taking a toll on all of us. I would always be cleaning the house because this was my outlet. I cooked all meals and cleaned so much. I honestly was losing interest in being his woman. At this point, I hardly like to have any sexual contact with him. We had been together for ten years. I was not happy, and I knew my kids weren't either.

It was my niece's first communion celebration. My dad had come from Guatemala to be a part of the ceremony. Everyone had been drinking and having a good time. My husband asked me to dance, and I told him I was tired. Later on, my dad asked me to dance, and since he was visiting from Guatemala, I got up and danced with him. Around midnight once the restaurant closed we all decided to continue the party at my sister-in-law's house. We decided to stop by our house to change clothes. My mom had taken my kids with her. The minute we got to the house he began to question me, if I was embarrassed by him. I had no idea what he was talking about. But he was upset that I had danced with my dad and not him. This made him think I was embarrassed by him. This was silly to me, everyone was family and knew he was my husband. I have no idea what got into him that night, but I immediately called my sister in law to pick me up before the storm broke down. He kept talking nonsense, and I grabbed an iron and told him that if he laid hands on me, I would hit him with the iron. I also told him I would call the cops. My sister in law got to my house, and I grabbed the car keys and ran out. I was crying and scared, but I was out the house. We left and went to her house about thirty minutes later I heard my husband screaming out on the street. One of his friends had taken him there. He came to my brother's house and started to argue with me. He wanted me to give him the car keys, but I knew he was not okay to drive, so I refused. My dad was in the room. My brother and sister in law were in the living room telling him to calm down. He kept getting angrier as I refused to give him the keys. He kicked me and pushed me. My sister in law yelled at my brother to defend me I immediately got up because they pushed one another, and I didn't want this to get any bigger so, I gave him the car keys, and he left the house.

A few minutes later I hear a commotion outside. I decided to look what was going on. He was trying to take my kids with him. I was so angry and in disbelief that he would put our kids lives in danger. He was too drunk to know any better. We were all able to talk him out of it, and he finally left.

I slept at my brother's house that night. At this point, I knew that was the end of my marriage because he had the nerve to kick me in front of my brother and his wife. I knew that it was out of control and that if I didn't get out then, it would be too late.

I returned home the next day and did not talk to him. He allowed a few days to pass by then he forced himself unto me. I felt disgusted, and as soon it was all over I told him he needed to leave the house. Our marriage was over. He didn't take it too lightly. But he knew, this time, it was real. He slept on the couch for about two weeks before he finally got his things and moved out.

I remember this day vividly. I was at my son's T-ball graduation party when he called me and told me that he had taken all his things. I knew I would have to announce the news to my five-year-old son and my eight-year-old daughter. Before we went back home, and they would see the house without his belongings. It was one of the hardest things I had to do.

He would pick them up on weekends and cry to them that he missed his family. My daughter developed hatred towards me. Her grades soon dropped tremendously. She was always getting into trouble with her fifth-grade teacher. My son was only five, so it didn't affect him as much. What made it worse at that time was that I had just started a new job, and I was getting off till seven o'clock. This was one of the hardest times of my life. Not only did I have a new job but, my daughter was going through a real hard time adjusting without daddy at home.

I had my mom's support and help. She would pick up my kids from school and take care of them until I got home. I would only get about an hour to see them because they had a scheduled bedtime. I would cry daily. I was falling apart but was not able to show anyone my emotions. I knew that in the end this would be the best decision for everyone. If I could only survive these tough times, then it would all be worth it. No matter how hard it got, I made a decision not to talk bad to my kids about daddy. I knew that they would need him in their lives. I was mentally a mess and broken inside and out, but I knew that one day the pain would go away and that I had made the right choice to get out before it was too late.

As I look back in time, I thank God every day for giving me the courage to walk away just in time. I have learned the importance of bringing awareness into the community. Domestic Violence is more common than we want to believe. So many people are suffering internally, and not many are informed properly. Domestic violence is a repetitive action from the abuser to the victim. They abuser needs to have power and control over the victim.

I learned that it impacts the life of the victim and the victim's children throughout their life. Most of my relationships after my marriage were toxic. I always wanted to be in control of any situation. In many cases, victims become abusers in other relationships. For example, my daughter was abusive with her classmates, and I never understood it was a consequence of what she had witnessed at home. Had I known the importance of counseling I would had taken her so she could cope with the anger she had inside. She had seen mom and dad fight and "make up" for years. This is what is known as "The Cycle of Violence."

The cycle consists of three phases:

1. The tension building phase: This is when tension builds up between couples due to many reasons, such as problems regarding jobs, finances, children, and other areas are stressors that increase tension. There may be verbal, emotional, or physical abuse during this phase.
2. The acute battering incident: This is an uncontrollable discharge of the built-up tension. The type of battering that occurs is usually much more serious and intense than in phase one, and the victim may be severely injured.
3. The honeymoon phase: This is when the kindness and love behavior comes along and when promises are made, and gifts are given. Ironically in this stage, the couple bonds and the relationship strengthens their commitment but slowly fades.

The duration of each phase varies between and within couples. The cycle is then repeated.

Love does not hurt anybody. It's important to love yourself and be whole before entering any relationship. I learned the hard way that being rebellious to my mother and entering a relationship hurt me more than I could ever imagine. I had two beautiful children out of this rebellious love but hurt them along the way too. Children deserve to be in a loving home. It's important to seek help and not to be ashamed. It's okay to take all the time needed to allow every wound heal properly Everyone deserves to love and be loved properly.

# Survival Talk...

# The Love of a Mother/Father

Parenting is not easy. However, understanding that there will be parenting challenges and trials along the way we must do our best to go the distance to provide our children with a safe, balanced, healthy lifestyle; so that the child has a fair opportunity for a successful life.

*The Presence of a Father/Mother helps to give a child ...*
☐ *Sense of Stability*
☐ *Sense of Protection*
☐ *Sense of Self-Love and Independence*
☐ *Support*
☐ *Truth*
☐ *Honor*
☐ *Respect*
☐ *Inspiration*
☐ *Unconditional Love*
☐ *Positive Reassurance*
☐ *Instruction*
☐ *Communication*
☐ *Accountability*
☐ *Moral Character*

When one or both parties in a relationship have never actually experienced the connection of a mother's or father's love, there may be relationship challenges. However, if we begin to heal through our pain, we can patiently love in spite of our wounded past.

Did you grow up with or without a father/mother in the home?

How do you feel it affected you as a child? ...as an adult?

If you are currently raising children without a father/mother, how does the situation impact their lives?

If you could change anything about your relationship with your dad/mom, what would it be?

# Chapter Nine

## MAN-CHILD OF MY PAIN
### By Evangelist Janat'e M.A. Ingram

*"Evangelist"*

*The Calling God Placed on My Life!*

**Evangelist** – *one who proclaims the good news.*

**Evangelism** – *proclaiming the gospel to those that have not heard or received it.*

*"And He gave some, Apostles; and some, prophets; and some, **evangelists**; and some pastors and teachers; for perfecting of the saints, for the work of the ministry, for the edifying of the body of Christ: Till we all come in the unity of the faith, and the knowledge of the Son of God, unto a perfect man, unto the measure*

*Of the stature of the fullness of Christ." Ephesians 4:11-13*

It was foretold at the time of my birth that a special child would be born; a profit even informed my parents that I would speak truth to many. Even more so, that my life was already spoken for, and God has prepared a path for me that would be magnetic to those who I encounter. Indeed, even as a child, I heard the voice of Christ, yet was unable to answer it.

136

I remember when I first heard his voice, I was about six years old, my parents were separated, and I was moved to Alabama with my mother's Sister, her husband and 5 children. This part of my family was born and raised nothing but "country", and it was impossible to hide it. After a series of abusive nights and lonely days filled with my cousin touching me, and putting his long black private part in my mouth, as if I knew what to do with it. I prayed that God would take me back to Buffalo with my father, at least until my mother finished college. The answer came in the form of a phone number, a number that I learned before I left home, my grandparents, (716) 855-06**. Hearing my grandfather's voice was such an inviting feeling, I knew God heard me when I asked him to take me away from the pain and lack of love I was receiving.

Yet, to this day, I recall that phone number that I was able to remember by God's grace. I believe that my brief stay in that horrible place was just early signs that showed me how to asked God to get involved, and trust that he will handle the situation. I will never really understand how a grown man could take the innocents of a young woman, away with no regards to the damages made by his strength. Even so, he will never know the trust that was lost due to him treating me as if I was a woman, his woman, a nasty woman.

I was never negative about my mistreatment; I told my family that I was entrusted with, I was more comfortable being with people I knew. I told my new found family that I was thankful for letting me stay with them, but, I really missed my dad. And my mother who attended Alabama State University, who might have felt betrayed, yet I assured her that God wanted me to go back home, it was her time to leave, not mine.

## Life's Recovery Room of ...

I gave them life, multiple cells entered me, and I made them one, related, yet still unrelated. Like Able and Cain with Isaac and Jacob too, my son's bloodlines are so unique. Their tones and shades of Blackness that denotes they are mine, shared with missing Adams or Fathers, yes more than one, I gave birth to four sons to be exact, and I became the image of Eve's sin.

My oldest son is 23 and the result of childhood lust and teenage thrust of "baby daddy" drama. Me the student that had to finish high school, yet I was scared to admit that keeping my baby was a "Tupac" poster that no young woman wants to admit is embarrassingly cool. I mean I fit the part. I had a baby like Brenda in the song, "Brenda's gotta Baby, but, Brenda barley gotta brain, a damn shame, that girl can hardly spell her name". But, I was willing to carry a silly mockery of a nickname just to fit in. It was said that I disappointed my family in such an unroyal way. When the weekends would come, I recall times when my son was one-year-old. I was chasing his father in unknown cars, pulling up as if this would make him take part in the life of our child.

At that time, I could care less if the trunk was loaded with drugs and money, I did not mind being renamed once again to fit how

I was acting. The slap to my face, from me spitting in his, was minimal to the time he dragged me on the side of a moving car. Yikes, the first son saw fights of all sorts, from high school to graduation, from my house to his father's hole in the wall, all the way back to his father's mother's dwelling. I fought so much; I didn't care to focus on loving him, and his Adam loved the streets more than we. The Bible tells us to raise up a child in the ways in which he will go, and he will not depart, well, in this case, our work was cut out for us, concerning my first son.

Ten years later I almost lost my mind to the announcement that I again was pregnant; I was introduced to abusive intimacy, and I liked it. We would meet in a parking lot, and have a conversation that made it seem as if the world was at my fingertips, and he was the worth the touch. Then in the dark rooms of lust, we created a space of pain for pleasure. I was his pounding board, and I felt as if I deserved it because after all, you can't' tell me my name isn't "bitch." See I had the pleasure of desiring sex this way because on numerous times it had been taken from me and his love was no different until; his love gave me seed. It grew to a young man, and the young man grew to have fits, and I allowed his Adam interfere by beating him. He couldn't express his changes to anyone, not even me; he dealt him beatings for secrets exchanged, and his father was like an Adam, who could have killed everything in the garden, as long as he was still left in control. I wish I could recall the moment's lust took control and call them wonderful. The truth is I recall them to be a lie of Love.

They all ended with a Kiss, a reminder that this is what a man-child and his mother needed with the absence of Adam in the house.

As I sit here in the Recovery Room, my last episode replays in my head, "the back room window shattered as I said no more to the abuse to my body and my child, my mind and soul says, "No." His hands assured me that "No" was not a suitable answer. With the strength of my family, the hits became void, and would only revisit when my need to have the Adams return and with hopes, he provides what a father would provide for the child. My son is now a 13-year old young man and the encounters with him, and his father is slim to none. As my son began to regroup from the anger the abuse from his father caused, and we talked more, I realized that by my child was made from Lustful pain thru me, and I failed then to protect him.

My hands were the epidemic of what most women avoid; they were weapons of Love Wars. I loved and hated love all at the same time, it became a pattern to fight my partner, he would cheat, and I would fight. 12 years ago, my lover was a rebel and a provider; we had a child in love and called him a Loyal Survivor, yet, the love and the hustle we shared was not enough. He insulted me, me a stay at home mom who covered for him while he worked I sold the liquor, the weed, the guns, and Soda Machine. And I felt like the house he purchased and kept in his name was all for the building of our child and us, and my two children from prior Adams, and his one son. Yet, when his mother became hopelessly unable to live on her own, he moved her in. Prior to this, we were the image of a family on the move. Heck, we even purchased a building to open several businesses. But then as they worked I returned to school. And the grind continued because our customers were put on a schedule that avoided mother.

Yet, the strife of having an overseer was just too much. She saw our love as a lie and proceeded to paint a picture that showed me as the one who was in the wrong. His nights became long; his respect became little to none. My postpartum frustration was filled with rage towards him, his mother and his new found side chick. Yes, I had allowed the fight to win again, and I held nothing back except my heart because it was truly finding a way to mimic concrete mixtures with no shape.

Once the house was empty, and the memories filled each room so much so that the Adam of lust and pain was allowed back in to numb me weekly. I knew it was time to go; even my body desired not to feel the thrust of a fist or an angry penis anymore in this season of life. So, I would fit comfort in the smoke until Adam 4 came, had me open with a mindset of freedom, Woodstock living. Yes, the sexual freedom of having what you want as long as you knew if would not last always, and if it did, more of your was required.

You would think that I learned a lesson, that I had given up on love, but this Adam, he gave me a dance, and I gave him me freely, lies of love once known and a relationship filled with even more lies. But he became my first husband, him as Adam made me legally EVE.

Even though we were together, I raised my sons, pretending that we lived less so royal, when we really just existed. For the most part, this Adam of a man gave me liberty, unlike the others who just planted their seed, while leaving me to make sure it grew. He gave me whatever I wanted, especially if it didn't make him put his life on hold and his lies on "Blast".

I found out about his lies, as they were molded in the image of a classmate of ours who we graduated College with. I had a notion that she had the hots for him, and I even wanted to believe his lies about their friendship. But, when I saw him and his mistress together, in our new van (which we were losing our home to keep), I fought her and tried to hurt her too… Yes, I did. He was busted, and I tried to beat them to a pulp because he was my "husband" they were my "friends", we had just graduated together, and I had child number 4, but no one had loyalty. That's what I believed, so I fought, and he tried to hold me, we fought more, but, this time, I moved on. Leaving our seed with them since it looked as if they liked playing happy family.

Months went by, and my divorce was finalized. Within almost a year that feeling came again, that inner feeling that visited me when I was praying to come back to Buffalo. I prayed and asked God to locate my son, and quickly I saw a vision of a house and address. I asked an officer friend of mine just to follow me in case the house was wrong, or worsts, The day I found my youngest son, he was sitting in a house filled with smoke, and strange people, I weep, took him, and that day prepared to move out of Buffalo to Petersburg, Virginia. What an opportunity it is to leave your hometown and start over! And that is just what happened, I wanted for love, still. I never wanted LOVE to end in a fight. I wanted love to be pure and new.

So, at the end of my adventures in Virginia, I gave in to the chase of another man, one that supported my 3.5-year journey. This countrified man took my life on a roller coaster ride from the time I moved to the "Burg," till I left. But for some reason stuck it out and we made moves selling food, and when he had the stroke, I convinced him to move to my hometown and cook his great food. We did it, we went back home, we meaning me, him and years of hidden abuse and distrust, a wall that guarded my heart, yet longed for true love and my 3 youngest sons, as the older one turned his pain into a jail sentence of two years, and he was released the day I got back to Buffalo.

We all found a place to dwell, me back in radio at the station where I made history breaking promotions, him with a job and his grill part time, my hidden abuse found comfort in smoking weed and being with old friends and family. This quickly turned into arguments as his job was lost, and his money was gone. His laziness surfaced and memories of abuse from 6 years old till that day, that day where I blocked, and he punches, I punched, and he punched harder. I yelled, and my children cried, they cried, and I hurt. A vicious cycle if you ask me. On that day, I realized what I had inherited and never dealt with. Maybe it was the concussion he gave me, maybe it was the cocaine I found in my bed.

Years of pacifiers which I wished would be that love, not of pain. I created the image of what a man was, an outline of everything my father wasn't and some of that he was. I decided to build my communication and calling, no longer allowing men to wear their hands on my body in forms of lust, adulterous wounds or scars. Yes, I felt if I could have a lover that would be that testimony of change as I saw in my father, I too could be loved. My stepmother seemed to endure love, and I wanted to embrace the love that my real mother lost.

Fast Forward 3 years…

But this wasn't conditional love that was based on comfort and convenience, a tired friendship that was born of a lie, and I lived a curse and was blinded until I got into the recovery room. Here I lost loved ones that were dear to me; my 26-year-old brother "decided" to die in a fire. I say he "decided" because he poured out so much prior to leaving this earth that his death brought me life. Him dying resounded in my head and pierced a hole in my heart that Only God could repair. That day, I told Elohim, "If you give me PEACE thru this Lord, I will serve you.

My Brother's death reminded me that; I was saved; I had no need to fight like a warrior. He told me my love was attentive and true. That I could conquer this city and beyond if I would stop allowing people to dictate what worked for me and just live. His death left me with his woman, a young white woman who didn't realize she was not allowed to use the N-word, and that she was a special gift to our family, because of the love she had for my brother.

With her love and encouragement, I was able to confront my past and say goodbye to all the heartache, pain lies, loneliness, and misery. Her voice was soft and sweet, and she held my brother's memory dear, and we would stay up night after night and speak about how to move forward. With no real commitment in my life, I was in a place where I divorced and found out I was never in a legal marriage, I rejoiced!

Still, with a desire to be a wife, yet this time in the season and without the baggage. I've learned to be very clear on needs when praying. I asked for "Someone who loves God 1st and is patient enough to heal me from my losses (No Matter How Long It Takes). Stable, non-violent and had no addiction to drugs. Handsome and tall, willing to work and work with me, I was even bold enough to ask that he not be a stranger to me, have no children and willing to spoil me. Ok with starting from the bottom, and building a family, meaning he has to be the best example to my boys. Not an Adam, but a King…"

It's funny because no one ever wants to be alone, we all desire to be loved and looked after. Now when this tall, fine man walked onto my job at the college, we knew each other; I had a crush on him in 3rd grade. He remembered me and his speech was still "Oh, so cute."
When he asked me to go for a walk and catch up on old times, I

accepted. Then he disappeared for months and forgot about him, then out of nowhere the week of my Brothers funeral, I answered his phone call, and again he asked about the walk I had said yes too, and he held me to it. It was brief and to the point, and we have walked together for over one year now. But this walk was just a walk. Some dates took place, and I found this man to be a friend and of the same belief, so it was best to leave it right there as I am being prepared for my King. With no rush to run into courtship or marriage, God kept his promise of PEACE, and I have been taking the steps to serve God, commit to his will 1st and heal.

I am now taking time and welcoming encouragement to make sure that the Curse of Adam is gone. I wait for the day I am totally capable of knowing love and having love hold me without offering bruises. Not pain, just him, not my past and the urge to fight, but him, my Adam, who with a longing to hold hands, walk, talk and receive hugs he is all mine.

In time, I found that PEACE gave me "LOVE." And that is the Love I must pour out to my sons, as they are the Man - Child of my Pain.

# Survival Talk...

## Wisdom

God will use whatever he wants to display his glory.

A season of suffering is a small assignment when compared to the reward. Your problems, struggles, and pain all have a purpose. Rather than be angry about the things that you have gone through, explore it. Ponder it. Use it to the glory of God.

What does the word "wisdom" mean to you?
Explain how your life's experiences have shaped your views of wisdom?

Understand that the wounds of your reality were meant for a purpose.
–Wisdom

# Chapter Ten

## USING THE BRICKS OF LIFE TO BUILD YOUR THRONE! QUEENS
By Jenni Steele

*1. Be true to yourself! 2. You owe it to yourself... 3. Forgive yourself and move forward!*

Confidence is in the root of your soul. I am often asked how are you so strong today? How can you speak with such strength and confidence? Why do you not hate men for what you went through? How are you able to speak in depth about your life? What has made you the woman you are today? Do your children know what you went through?

Yes, I experienced domestic violence as a teenager when I should have been enjoying and learning about life. Feeling love for the first time! The butterflies and excitement of what love feels like. It was one of the most traumatic experiences of my life. A feeling you never forget! As the saying goes you will forget what was said but you will never forget how someone made you feel. Ain't that the truth! If my neighbor were not so nosey, it's possible I may not be here today.

When the person you love turns on you and you are unable to see it for what it is, it's because we are blinded by love, the hurt, the pain, and the loneliness of your thoughts and fears with nowhere to turn. Who would believe that this charming man would ever lay his hands on you? Threaten you? The truth is, It's not your secret. It's his secret that you are hiding. Protecting him and thinking that I can help him to change his behavior. This will be the last time as he cries in the corner with his head in his hands. We were Bonnie and Clyde against the world because as this relationship was ending I had no close friends or family around me, and I was a nervous wreck! No confidence and in a dark place. Have you ever walked on eggshells?

Think about it!


The last time I left my home by ambulance knowing that could have been the end, finding the courage not to go back behind those closed doors again. Having the strength to rebuild because when it gets tough, that's when you have to deal with your emotions. Your heart may be broken and you may drawback the tears as you begin piecing your life back together piece by piece like a jigsaw puzzle. This is when you need your friends and family the most.

I am here today, and I give thanks for that because it was not my time to go. I was given a second chance at life. A chance to change the cycle that many families don't even realize they are involved in. A chance to teach my children about love, healthy and unhealthy relationships. Something noone sat down and spoke to me about. Being a parent is more than washing, cooking, and cleaning. We have a responsibility to educate and to teach, as well as practice what we preach.

In life, I have learned that we must not be afraid to get help and support. I received counseling but many people are scared and do not see it through because it opens us up  childhood memories; the good, the bad, and the ugly. We have to accept the truth about ourselves, our families and our past.  Every family has secrets both good and bad. We have to face the responsibility and take charge of what is next. Many of us are not ready for this experience, but the truth is, if you do not start to deal with your feelings, then they will live with you for the rest of your life! If you do not get the right support, any relationship you have will be scarred and may be stagnant emotionally. A mind is a powerful tool because it can enslave us, or make us happy and we must use it wisely.

Forgiving him for what he put me through was my first step on this path of rebuilding my confidence. I had to listen to what he said his reasons were. That included his childhood, his "whys," and his "ifs, ands and butts." I think it is time to learn how to dissect how the cycle begins and how we can stop it from continuing through the next generation. It was never going to be easy. In court, he shared parts of his childhood. The learned behavior and patterns. If we are going to be the change, we must understand the depth of the change we are about to create.

There are many people living with trauma and rooted feelings and memories. Some try to forget and bury them deep within. But like everything  that sinks to the bottom, it will at some point rise to the top!

I was at my lowest point. I was scared. I did not know who I was. I was lost. I did not know what kind of woman I was going to be. Can I get back on the right track? Over the years as I started to build back my strength I knew that what I went through was going to change me. Change the way I raise my children. What I did not know was how strong it was going to make me. How was I going to motivate myself back on track? What does not kill you makes you stronger. There is so much truth in that quote it is unreal!!

*My Reality No1*

Learning to love yourself again and to unlearn everything that you have been taught is one of the hardest challenges you will face. Acceptance of our journey and to understand you are not to blame is the first step. Until you accept what you have been through, you will not be able to move on by getting help and support or talking through your feelings and fears.

This may make you angry, sad and upset, but this is normal. We have to release these feelings in order to start to heal the wounds that we have rooted so deep in the mind. Remember that powerful tool I mentioned earlier? Many of us will risk everything to keep these feelings rooted. You owe it to yourself to be true to yourself so you can move on and live a happy and rewarding life.

I have spent many years out of relationships in between breakups. Why? Because I needed to understand what was learnt, where it went wrong, my strengths and my weaknesses. Do you know yours? Be honest! Why not make a list of them. It will give you a chance to measure your own growth.

Take a moment to list your strengths and weaknesses in the space provided below:

| STRENGHTHS | WEAKNESSES |
|---|---|
|  |  |
|  |  |
|  |  |
|  |  |
|  |  |
|  |  |
|  |  |

Sharing my traumatic past with my children was important to me. I told them as early as I could when I felt they were ready. Which was during their teenage years. It was important for them to understand healthy & unhealthy relationships as siblings first. No shouting, hitting, punching or disrespecting of me, their father or each other. In turn, it was easier to teach them about the opposite sex. The cycle I spoke of earlier will continue unless we make a change in the right direction. As a teenager I hid the truth from the world. I only showed them what I wanted them to know, or see, and to be honest, it was easy! Too easy. I wanted my children to be honest with me. Even if they wanted to lie, they wouldn't or couldn't. I wanted a bond with them like no other. I had always been honest with them even when we never had a lot of money. They know me to have 2 jobs and work hard for everything we have. And in turn, they work hard for what they have. We can appreciate what we prayed for. For what we now have...

I wanted to raise champions. When the going gets tough we draw from the strength we have inside, face our fears and keep going, We push each other. I never had a close relationship with my family. Being young, living so far away from everyone. My challenge with my children was breaking that very cycle. That truth I spoke of earlier, that families don't even realise they are in because honestly my family distances growing up meant we never really had a close family set up. So as a child I never had the family closeness in times of need. Cycles are all around us. Many of us will never see them until we truly understand ourselves and face the reality.

## My Reality No 2

Being comfortable in your own skin. Do you love yourself enough? Do you celebrate your success and achievements? How far have you come?

We must try not to be so hard on ourselves. We have come a long way. Try and think about how far you have come instead of how much further you have to go! Success is a journey, and a mindset. Remember that powerful tool we spoke about earlier? Sit down and remember to find a peaceful moment and remember where you was last year, the year before. How far have you come? Give yourself a round of applause and smile...

*My Reality No 3*

Don't let anybody stop you from being who you want to be, having the career or business you want. The only person that can stop you is YOU! Yes You!! It takes strength, dedication and belief in yourself to have success in life, business and love. Nobody said it was going to be easy, as there is no book on life and what to expect. We will all have different paths and journeys. The one thing we all have in common is a powerful tool. The mind. And it will control you if you let it! It will guide you on how to act and feel if you use it wisely.

*My New Chapter*

I never stopped raising the topic of domestic violence, healthy and unhealthy relationships. And most importantly dissecting the learned behavior that keeps the cycle going. Turning a negative experience into a positive solution over the years has given me the greatest strength to be the best I can be. Guiding and supporting my children to be the best they can be. Helping and supporting others is part of my daily makeup and I would not change it for the world.

The encouragement and support that I continue to receive from my community and around the world has been amazing. This is what motivates me to motivate others. When I stood up for what I believed in 20 years ago, I never imagined what my life would become; the success that I have been blessed with today.

Today I am a mother of three champions, a glamorous "GlamMa," an award-winning successful business woman, The National Ambassador of Domestic Violence UK, Broadcast Journalist, and Entertainment Correspondent. I produce Entertainement News every week live on radio. I create and deliver programs and support others personally through their experiences and signpost them to support services. I raise awareness of Healthy, Unhealthy, and Domestic violence relationships and support parents on educating their teenagers about relationships. In February 2015, I launched The Jenni Steele Foundation, my legacy that supports, educates and motivates the next generation of leader's boys and girls through creative programs.

As I became a woman, I learned that healthy and happy relationships help us to feel better about ourselves. Unhealthy relationships make us feel unhappy and unsafe. If you FEAR your partner, you need to speak to someone. Today!

What is my secret? I went against the grain, and I still go against the grain with every challenge I face. I have dealt with some home truths and to this day I still deal with home truths. I have made mistakes, and I learn from them as they are the real test in how far we have come. I can look in the mirror and know that I am in charge of my destination, and if I choose happiness then that is what I must get! I stand for: honesty, equality, kindness, compassion, treating people the way I want to be treated and helping those in need. To me, those are my values. Hard work and determination are the keys. I no longer ask permission because I am on a mission. When you learn, you teach.

The truth is YOU can become as GREAT as YOU want to be! YOUR confidence is in the root of your SOUL. dig deep my Queen. Dig deep! Get support and guidance and use the bricks of life to rebuild your Throne!

Just Remember: On your journey to building back your confidence after a traumatic experience, don't be so hard on yourself. Remember we must build on our strengths with determination. You don't just wake up strong... Just like training in the gym, building on your strength takes time and plenty of effort.

I know what it is like to have noone and nowhere to turn. If you thought you had noone when you started this book, you now have ME...

The Lioness x

# Survival Talk...

# Goal Setting

Goal setting and proper planning will help you to move forward with your life goals. Mind, body and soul.

**Goal setting is vital to your growth and wellness!**

If you don't know where you are going, *how will you ever know when you get there?*

As you begin to take the time to consider your future, writing or journaling each goal will help you to begin to see the vision. Then, once the vision is realized, you will begin to take action to manifest it. Vision takes confidence. Planning requires action.

Moving forward in a greater direction should always encourage us to reach higher. Just think of learning to ride a bicycle. Initially, there is a vision which is followed by an action. Though there is a chance that you may fall—becoming wounded—you can still build up enough courage to try it until you have achieved.

AFFIRMATION

*Today, I will plan my goals and take action so that I reach my next level.*

It's time to move forward with your future goals. Career goals, educational goals, spiritual goals, etc… You must do this in spite of the past. In spite of the negative comments or actions of others.

What are your goals?

What are you plans for achieving your goals?

What are the challenges that you feel may interfere with the achievement of your goals?

How will you celebrate your accomplishment?

Visualize your plan and put it into action – *your life depends on it.*

# Chapter Eleven

## WHAT'S LOVE GOT TO DO WITH IT?
### By Tameeka Manuel

This woman has fought a thousand battles and is still standing. Has cried a thousand tears and is still smiling. Has been broken, abandoned and rejected but still she walks proud, laughs loud, lives without fear, and loves without a doubt. This woman is beautiful. This woman is humble. THIS WOMAN IS ME!

I remember like it was yesterday, It was January 2004, what was supposed to be a short trip to Georgia, ended up being a flight to my new residence. I caught a flight from Buffalo, NY to Atlanta, Georgia to visit a relative. With the crime rate rising at a rapid pace back home in Buffalo and having three children to look after, it was imperative that I found somewhere a little more "kid friendly" to raise my children. By the looks of things, Georgia appeared to be the "perfect" place to begin a new life and expose my children to greater opportunities than what they had in Buffalo. Therefore, without much thought, Georgia became our new home. Although I had no income when I first moved to Georgia, I had a God-given talent and a plan. I decided to begin styling hair in my home to earn money until I was able to find a position in a salon. Since I was already a licensed hairstylist, I knew how to style hair, but since my cosmetology license was issued in New York State, I could not use it in Georgia. While working on earning my Georgia State Cosmetology License, I worked from my home as a temporary alternative. I earned my license within a few months and after browsing a few direct mailing advertisements, I found employment working at a local beauty salon making excellent money.

It was not easy trying to work at a hair salon full-time and raise three children without any assistance. I spent the first few months racing home to get the kids off of the school bus, make them something to eat and sometimes bring them to the salon with me. Some days were easy while other days were a challenge. There were days where I would show up late to get them off of the bus, and they would just sit on the porch and wait for me to arrive. However, I was determined to "work my plan and make my plan work." I refused to go back home as a failure and more importantly, I refused to raise my children in Buffalo, New York. The owner of the salon where I was working introduced me to a friend of hers who happened to babysit for a living. I hired the babysitter to pick my children up after school and sit with them until I made it home from the salon.

Within a year's time, all of my hard work and dedication was clearly paying off. In April 2005, I was blessed to open my first hair salon on the south side of Atlanta. In the back of my salon, I had a room for my children to spend time while I worked. Shortly after opening my salon, I was also blessed to move into a new house that was more suitable for my family. Before the move, while I was packing, I took a short break to cook dinner for my children. My next door neighbor's daughter was at my house at that time to help me pack. I recall that she stepped out on my porch for a minute to speak with her cousin who just stopped by her house. Although I did not see what her cousin looks like I told her to tell him "hello." Before I knew it, we were on the phone talking, and we ended up exchanging numbers so that we can talk again. Later that evening he called me as promised, and we hit it off immediately. We got through all of the icebreakers and spoke about everything under the sun from favorite colors to politics. Although I was not interested in politics, I listened to what he had to say because he made everything he spoke about seem so interesting. The conversation went on for at least two hours. From that first night, there was an instant mental attraction, and I could not wait to meet him. I could not believe that I could hold a two-hour conversation with someone whom I just informally met and had never seen "face to face." I was impressed by his extensive vocabulary, his intelligence, the fact that he was well traveled, and more importantly, he was God-fearing, which was a plus in my eyes. After the first phone call, we talked on the phone every day until we would fall asleep.      During one of our daily conversations, he informed me that he would be coming back to Georgia and would love to meet me. I was so excited that I could not wait to lay my eyes on him. I prayed that he would be the "tall, dark and handsome" man that I always dreamed of. Needless to say, we set up a date for us to meet.

On the day that we were scheduled to meet I was waiting for him arrive at my salon to pick me up. Although we had scheduled a date to go out for dinner, I wanted him to meet me at my place of business just in case he was a psychopath. Not literally, but this was a necessary precaution that my friends and I had whenever we met new guys and were headed out for first dates. We always asked a plethora of questions and someone would "slip out" jot down the license plate number of the gentleman's car "just in case." As I was waiting, I saw a guy in a car pull up in front of the salon, and I instinctively knew it was him. However, he was nothing like I had imagined but I told myself that I was going to allow myself to think outside of the box and release my "tall, dark and handsome" expectations. Besides, I was already won over by his conversation and intellect. After meeting all of my friends, we left for our first date. During the date, I was impressed by his demeanor. He showed me that chivalry still existed. He opened doors, pulled out my chair, and his table etiquette was on point. By the end of the date, we both agreed that we would like to see each other again.

After four months of talking on the phone and seeing each other every day I decided to allow him to meet my children. We met in a parking lot at a Church, and I introduced him to my children as my friend. We made it seem as though we just happened to see each other in the parking lot. I did not want my children to feel uncomfortable. After church, we went to dinner and took the kids to the park. My children took a liking to him instantly. Things seemed to be falling into place. He began to spend time with my children while I was working; he would take them to the park just to get them out of the house. My children loved spending time with him.

However, it didn't take much time before he started to show signs of insecurity, jealousy, and controlling behavior. After a short six months, I decided to let him know that I wanted to slow things down and just be friends. His response to me was that he had "invested too much time" into our relationship and that the relationship would only be over once he said it was over. We went back and forth on the status of the relationship until he became overwhelmed by the conversation and decided to walk away. He was walking and yelling things that I couldn't quite make out, nor was I trying to understand. He jumped into his vehicle and skidded off. He was driving like a maniac. He didn't slow down at all and approached the speed bumps with a ferocity that made his truck shake somewhat out of control. I watched him and just shook my head, but I was relieved to see him leave. The way he was behaving I didn't know what he was going to do so I was happy that he was gone. He called me later that evening and asked if he could come over to discuss my decision and to see if there was any way that we could work things out. After sitting on the phone with him for at least an hour and a half with him pleading his case, I broke down and decided to let him come over. It was then that he convinced me to give him another chance.

This "relationship" continued on for another year. Throughout this time, the relationship was extremely toxic and at one point, I questioned if what I was going through was actually considered domestic violence because I wasn't scared of him, and I always fought him back. I really did want "out" of the relationship, but any mention of breaking up would turn into a physical altercation with him reminding me that he loved me "to death." His insecurities grew heavy, and any thought that I was trying to seek attention from another man in his presence would result in him inflicting physical pain in public places without anyone noticing. For example, he would do things like pinch my leg or my arm or give me the "side-eye" as to say "wait until we get in the car or to the house." Any of those gestures was the "cue" that there would be more "drama" to come once we were alone. There would also be physical altercations to the point where I would have to drive as far away as possible and stay in a hotel with my children for a few days to have some peace away from him. My children used to love staying in different hotels because it was "fun" for them; they just didn't quite understand what was really happening. I tried my best to hide the drama from my children and many times we would engage in "silent" altercations so the children could not hear what was actually happening.

You see, I did not consider myself a victim because I was never afraid of him. It took more than his verbal threats, hair pulling, psychological tactics such as locking me inside his house so that I couldn't leave while he was at work or driving me to secluded parks and taking my car keys while he taunted me for hours before he would give me my keys back to scare me but it never worked. It took more than having bottles thrown at me, breaking of my cell phones, and busting out my car windows for me to be afraid. But it was one particular incident that took a turn for the worse when I knew that I had enough. Either I was going to die, or he was going to die, but one of us had to go!

It was the 4$^{th}$ of July 2007, my children, and I were invited to a huge barbecue event. I did not invite my boyfriend because he was already attending a different barbecue and appeared to be enjoying himself. As I was getting dressed, I told him that I was going to take the kids to the cookout and to my surprise, he showed up at my house before I was able to leave without him. I was furious! I thought, "how dare he hang out all day, and I am not welcomed to his friend's barbecue, but he wants to jump in my vehicle and invite himself to come with me?" I did not want to start any problems, so I just told the children to get in my car so we could leave. I was determined not to let him kill my positive feelings about the evening.

During the party, the night appeared to be moving along just fine. There was good music, good conversation, and great liquor. All of the children in attendance were playing together, and this allowed the adults to enjoy themselves as well. But just like many other nights, he began to accuse me of flirting with someone. At that point, both of us had quite a few alcoholic beverages, so the argument between the two of us began to get heated until some of the house guests intervened and separated us. He walked away with a few of the guys, and I went on the back patio of the home with a few ladies.

Although I had a few drinks, I remember drinking the same drink the entire night because I didn't want to mix my alcohol. At some point in the evening, a young lady handed me a cup of alcohol. It wasn't the same drink that I had been drinking throughout the night, so it didn't take long before I started to feel sick. I am not sure what kind of drink it was, but one thing was for sure, it didn't agree with what I was drinking through the night. I became very sick, and I knew it was time to go home. But because he and I both had quite a bit to drink, he was still arguing with me (yes at me, I was too sick to deal with his drama any longer). I fussed back at him a little but I really just needed to get home and lay down. My friend decided to drive me home while her husband followed behind her with my guy friend in the car with him.

Once we finally made it to the house, I was feeble and light headed. I just kept saying to myself "what in the world was in that last drink?" I just wanted to lay down. I went into my bedroom and threw myself across the bed with all of my clothes on. I had no energy to shower just yet. As I was laying there, he started going back to accusing me of flirting at the party. He carried on about how a few guys at the party was looking at me. He told me that I must've known them or used to *talk to* one of them, and he went on and on with his allegations and threats. At some point while he was talking I dozed off. When I woke up, he was still talking. I was too tired to entertain him that evening. Before I knew it, he was sitting on top of me yelling in my face and began to strike me in the face. Somehow I managed to kick him off of the bed, and I thought that I went to sleep after an exchange of words once he picked himself up from the floor.

The next morning I did not remember much of what happened. To me, it was just another altercation, and since this was just the "norm" for us, I really didn't think much of it. He got up and prepared himself for work as though the incident from the night before had never occurred. Shortly after he left for work, I got out of the bed, walked into my bathroom, turned on the light, and was stunned at the reflection that I saw in the mirror. It was that precise moment that I realized that something awful happened the previous night, and it was not just another altercation. Things had gone too far this time. When I saw my face, I saw a black eye with bite marks on my face and neck. I was in a state of shock and had to sit down for a moment to figure out and remember exactly what really happened the night before.

It was almost like watching a movie as I sat in the bathroom stall trying to recap the events that took place the night before, but it all came to me one frame at a time. I slowly recalled the blows to my face and I remembered being burned with a cigarette lighter on my thigh for refusing to have sex with him. At that point, I became too angry to cry, and I felt ashamed that I allowed things in this relationship to get this far. As I was sitting in the bathroom collecting my thoughts, he returned to the house, came into the bathroom and asked me "What happened to your face? He kept yelling at me "Who did that to you?" I then looked at him and told him "You did!" He continued to deny his actions and demanding the names of possible people that could have done this to me. He said that he would never hurt me like that, and if he were the cause of my injuries, he did not remember. He then began to apologize as he kept hugging me and saying that he didn't mean it. At that point, I knew that I was "done" and could no longer have him in my life. I told him to leave my house, and he left quietly. I pondered what my steps would be but convinced myself that I was too embarrassed to call the police, so I cleaned myself up, put on some makeup, threw on some sunglasses and went to work.

At that point in my life, I decided that "enough was enough" and that I no longer be in a relationship with this man. For many weeks after this incident, he continued calling every number he had for me leaving countless messages, showing up at my home and my place of business pleading for another chance to prove himself. However, I vowed to stand by my decision to leave the toxic relationship in my past and not to re-enter it.

But, after a month of being pursued and persuaded by him, I found myself accepting his phone calls once again. This time, however, it was different, and it wasn't long after I began speaking with him and allowing him back into my life that I decided that I really couldn't be happy or comfortable around him anymore. Every time he would make a sudden move, raise his voice, or drink too much I knew that it increased the probability of another physical altercation. I felt that if we didn't end this relationship that one of us would end up dead or in jail for seriously injuring the other. As a result, I terminated the relationship.

As usual, he did not accept my decision not to be in a relationship with him again, and he pursued me diligently. I really didn't know how I was going to get him out of my life, and it wasn't until I met a new guy who became a part of my life that he began to lessen his attempts to contact me. Although he periodically texted me taunting messages or telling me that he "missed me" and wanted to see me, I no longer felt threatened. Eventually, he stopped reaching out to me and left me alone to live in peace.

One of my biggest regrets is that I never pressed criminal charges against him. I believe that if I had done that, then many of the instances would have never occurred, and perhaps I could have found my sense of peace much earlier.

When I entered into my new relationships, my new boyfriend was part of a strong support system for me and stepped into the role of "protector." He vowed to protect me and never to allow anyone else to hurt me, but he had no idea how much work he had taken on and what he had signed up for. Because of my emotional scars, it was quite challenging for my new friend to get too close to me. When I first met my new friend he had no idea where I lived for at least two or three months because I was uncomfortable with sharing the information. Once he was able to spend the night he had to sleep on the couch, and within a few months I allowed him to sleep in the bed, but that is then where we both were able to see how damaged I was. There were many nights where I would fight in my sleep to the point my new boyfriend would make sure I knew that he was getting in the bed before he actually got in the bed. He had to learn not to pull the covers too hard, or do anything to make me feel uneasy and he would often wait until I was asleep to pray over me and then repeat the prayer in the morning. Eventually, I began to sleep peacefully, and I am so grateful to have someone like him to help me and stick around through it all without judgment.

It took many years for me to share my story because I never considered myself a "victim" because I wasn't afraid of my abuser. I fought back every time, so I didn't consider myself a victim. How could I be? The reality is that YES! I was a victim, and it is still considered domestic violence. Even if you are not afraid of your abuser it is still considered domestic violence if you fight back. It is still a violent and toxic relationship that you must escape. I would suggest to every woman or man if you are in this type of relationship that you GET OUT because it only gets worse. Abuse comes in many forms and is not always physical so know the signs and know that if you are in an unhealthy relationship, you must GET OUT! You must get out to receive the services you need to heal and to make positive changes in your life. You deserve it!

In the words of Tina Turner. What's love got to do with it? Love has everything to do with it because love does not hurt!

Be Blessed
Jameela
Manuel
Stay tuned for more

# Survival Talk...

# Recognizing Dating Violence

Research shows that the mass majority of those in abusive relationships were those that have experienced or witnessed some sort of abuse as a child. Sadly enough, many of those individuals viewed abuse as "normal" behavior or some even felt as though being abused was warranted...saying things such as:

"If he doesn't hit me, that means he doesn't love me or care."
"If he doesn't call me constantly to find out my whereabouts he doesn't care about me."
"If she doesn't argue with me, maybe she doesn't care."
"As long as he/she pays the bills, I can take it."

With that being said, relationship abuse has been noted as an on-going epidemic, generation-after-generation based on hurt and continual uninhibited thinking patterns. Seeing as though I too, have had my share of abuse within relationships, I can grasp ahold of how this can be construed as a plaguing effect. However, for me, it was being able to look back over my experiences, recognizing certain behavior to understand that abuse (verbal, emotional, physical, etc.) should not be a way of life. As we begin to form our forward opinions of relationships we must be able to identify the difference between a healthy relationship and a toxic relationship; being mindful and watchful for abusive traits.

## Toxic Relationship

- Controlling behaviors
- Verbal outbursts/arguing
- Name calling
 - Insulting
-Punishing
- Religious control
- Isolation from friends and family
- Sexual abuse
- Blaming
- Threatening
- Forcing any act without mutual consent.

## Healthy Relationship

- Loving
- Complementing
- Respectful
 - Affectionate
- Considerate
- Loyal
- Trustworthy
 - Encouraging
 - Inspiring
- Pleasurable
- Having Sense of Compassion
- Moral Character
- Easy Going
 - Not Forceful

Persuasion can be a form of abuse as well; which can be equally compared to controlling. The act of persuasion is usually used to influence or induce us to do things that are generally outside of our 'moral character'.

Many times in relationships, persuasion is used in situations that involve, drugs, alcohol sex or religion—all circumstances that can become very detrimental to our overall health and wellness. Persuasive abuse taps into our minds giving way into our inner emotion which helps our abuser to manipulate us into trying drugs, drinking, having sex with others or steering us into bondage under religion. Some even feel that sex after abuse is a way to persuade you to forgive and forget.

Oftentimes, your partner will be very apologetic after the abusive behavior. Attempting to do nice things or buy gifts. There are also times when your partner may become increasingly withdrawn, ignoring or blaming. In my opinion, the saying holds true ....if your partner uses a form of abuse against you once, they will, in fact, try it again (in the same or another form). Therefore, it is important to consult with a counselor, mentor or other care professional to begin to seek help immediately. Don't wait until it's too late.

Keeping in mind that family members, co-workers or friends may lend an ear, be careful when choosing someone to confide in about the details of your abusive situation. Though they may love or care about you, the truth is everyone is not equipped to offer safe, sound unbiased advice—not to say that they will not support you, just be aware how much you share so that you are clear in making your own choices.

# Chapter Twelve

## SLEEPING WITH THE ENEMY
### By Tamiko Lowry-Pugh

I remember watching the hit movie "Sleeping with the Enemy" starring the beautiful Julia Roberts back in 1991. In the movie, a young woman found herself having to fake her own death in order to escape her abusive husband. The husband was emotionally, mentally, and physically abusive. He also had an obsession with organizing his cupboards, and hand towels. He wanted everything to be perfect. Including his wife. I thought to myself; this would never happen to me. Fast forward 13 years later. I found myself in a very similar situation.

A few of my coworkers that were excitingly successful at finding great dates on a new Online Dating website insisted that I should try it out. They boasted about dates with nice men that led to great relationships; and ultimately to marriage. So, I decided to give it a try. So, I set up my Dating Profile Page. Then, about an hour later I received my first message from a guy. We chatted for a few days online before exchanging phone numbers. After talking on the phone and getting to know each other, I found out that he worked with one of my best friends. So I decided to give her a call to inquire about him. When asked she said *"Girl, he is your type."* Sealing the deal for the date, she went on to say that he was a nice guy, highlighting the good qualities that she knew of him. At first, I was kind of paranoid and apprehensive about going out with someone that I met online. But, since I got the 'OK' from my friend I felt that I was safe.

Of course, I was very impressed with how well the date went. As soon as I got home I deleted my Dating Profile Account. I thought for sure I met the man of my dreams. Things were moving fast. After dating for a few months, he met my children, and I met his. We became inseparable. Spending all of our free time together. We did family outings with our children. We were becoming a 'real family'.

The thing that attracted me and that I loved most about him was the way that he accepted my children who were from a previous relationship. He would always tell me that he felt that he was put in my life to take care of me. He also had this smile that would light up any dark room which also matched his infectious, outgoing personality. Everyone loved being around him. Not only that, but he was also a good provider and made me feel secure. The way that he would constantly compliment my looks and personality were also a plus.

Though enjoying the moment, things were really moving fast. About four months into the relationship we were having a general conversation when he looked over and said to me "Let's get married." Not too shocked by the question because of how good things were going, I said "OK." Happy, yet still playing in the back of mind were the times during the course of planning the wedding when I noticed that he would get angry and raise his voice at me. There were even times when he would talk to my children in a tone that I didn't like. But, I 'swept it under the rug' as him being stressed out because of the wedding plans and all of the changes that were taking place in our lives. A few months before the wedding we decided to start looking for a home that would accommodate our blended family. His children lived out of state, but they would visit us every other weekend and during certain holidays. He was very adamant making sure that we got the house that I liked. He wanted to make sure that I was happy and satisfied. Finally, we decided on a nice four bedroom home. We moved into the house three months before our wedding. I was indeed happy. I had my home, my family, and I was getting married for the first time in my life.

Soon after moving into our new home my fiancé began to talk to me as if I were one of the kids. He would yell at the children for no reason. He became very hostile and angry—all the time. His once loving tone of voice turned harsh and brash. What did I get myself into? He upsettingly became so mean that I was really starting to dislike him. Disturbed yet enabling, I justified and attributed his behavior to the stress of wedding planning.

As we got closer to the wedding date, the emotional and verbal outbursts began to get worse. He would walk around the house and not speak to me for days at a time. In the morning, as we would get dressed for work, he wouldn't speak to me or even say 'good morning.' Then, when I would say good morning to him, he would just look at me and roll his eyes. He began acting withdrawn, eerie and shared no regard for speaking to me in a very cold manner.

About two weeks before the wedding I began to have second thoughts, so I threatened to leave. He apologized for his behavior, convincing me to stay. As we got closer to the wedding date, my fiancé's attitude towards me got worse. He would look at me with disgust and roll his eyes at me. He would say things like…"You ain't all that." "I could do a lot better than you." But, because I had been engaged several times in the past I was too embarrassed to cancel this wedding. I sent the invitations out; my family booked plane tickets, and everyone was expecting a wedding.

The day of the wedding I maintained my composure, put on a fake smile and pretended to be happy. We looked each other in the eyes and said our vows like two people who were madly in love. We didn't even sleep together that night.

Over the course of the next three years my husband beat me emotionally, he beat me mentally, he beat me verbally, and he even beat me spiritually. He had been physical a few times by choking or restraining me. Although the physical abuse was not as often as the other forms of abuse, I feel that the emotional and verbal abuse had a bigger impact on me. It caused me to have a broken soul. Having a broken arm heals much faster than having a broken soul.

There are some things that I blocked out of my mind, and I do not remember. And some things are too painful to relive at this moment. I remember on several occasions being choked until I almost passed out. Thinking to myself, I'm about to die. But the most horrific incident was the day that I left. We were driving up the interstate, and I told him that I was leaving him for good. He got so angry that he forced the car to the side of the road where he began to hit, punch, and choke me. I think I passed out because the next thing I remember was being in the middle of the highway with cars swerving around me trying to prevent hitting me. Thankfully, someone saw what happened and called the police. I thought for sure I was going to die on that day. My life flashed before my eyes. I made it out, but not everyone does.

Trusting God and living according to Romans 8:28 has helped me to take my first steps on my path to survivorship. Everything that we go through in life has a reason and a purpose. Being able to turn my wounds into wisdom has given me strength and courage to live and to love again.

Since leaving my abuser, my life is full of freedom and peace. I am now living in my purpose of helping other women who are traveling the path that I survived! I am a full-time speaker, coach, and author, focusing on empowering women to live a life of passion, purpose, potential, and peace.

Are you sleeping with the enemy? If so, I encourage you to wake up before it's too late.

# Survival Talk...

# The Power of Loving Yourself

One of the most powerful lessons that I have learned throughout my life is that loving myself is very key to my happiness and emotional well-being. It is a fact that many people are not even aware of. Love is a powerful force in our lives and can be used to remedy many heartaches & pain. It gives us clarity of mind and motivation to be a better person. It helps us achieve greater things for ourselves—mind, body, and spirit.

Love Yourself!

Tamiko Lowry-Pugh

7 steps to begin loving yourself:

1. Get rid of negative influences
2. Take the time to do things that bring you joy
3. Step out of your comfort zone
4. Pray/meditate
5. Stop criticizing yourself
6. Be gentle, kind, and patient with yourself
7. Forgive yourself

# *Essential Wellness Principles to Help You Live a Winning Lifestyle*

Pray

Praise

Meditate

Eat Healthy

Exercise

Get Rest

Set Goals—Short Term & Long Term

Learn/Train/Study

Construct a Financial Plan to Help You Budget and Become a Good Steward Over Your Financial Blessings

Spend Quality Time with Friends & Family

Feed Your Spirit Good Energy

Take Time Out for Yourself

Explore New Opportunities

Be Mindful of Doing Things that You Like to Do vs. Just Those that You Have to Do

Explore Your Gifts & Talents

Smile/Laugh Often (*it soothes the soul*)

Speak Good Things into Existence in Your Life

Stay Positive/Surround Yourself with Positivity

*Realize that abuse is NEVER your fault.*
*Hurt people, hurt people; this is why healing from abuse is so*
*important to your wellness. It helps to prevent the cycle of hurt, abuse*
*and disparity.*

*(Proclaim that your life will never be the same)*

Survivorship is Real...

YOU SURVIVED!